Coloring Books for Grownups
# ALEBRIJES

# VISIT TODAY
# ILoveColoringBooksForAdults.com
# TO WIN A SET OF PREMIUM COLORED PENCILS

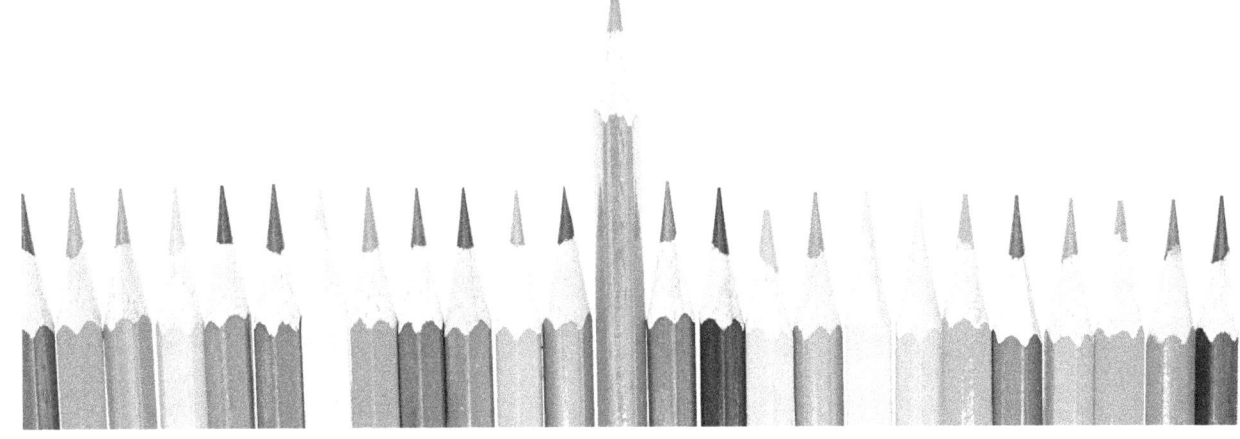

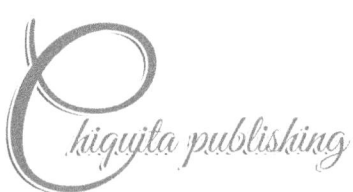
Chiquita publishing

Cover and page design by Cool Journals Studios - Copyright 2015

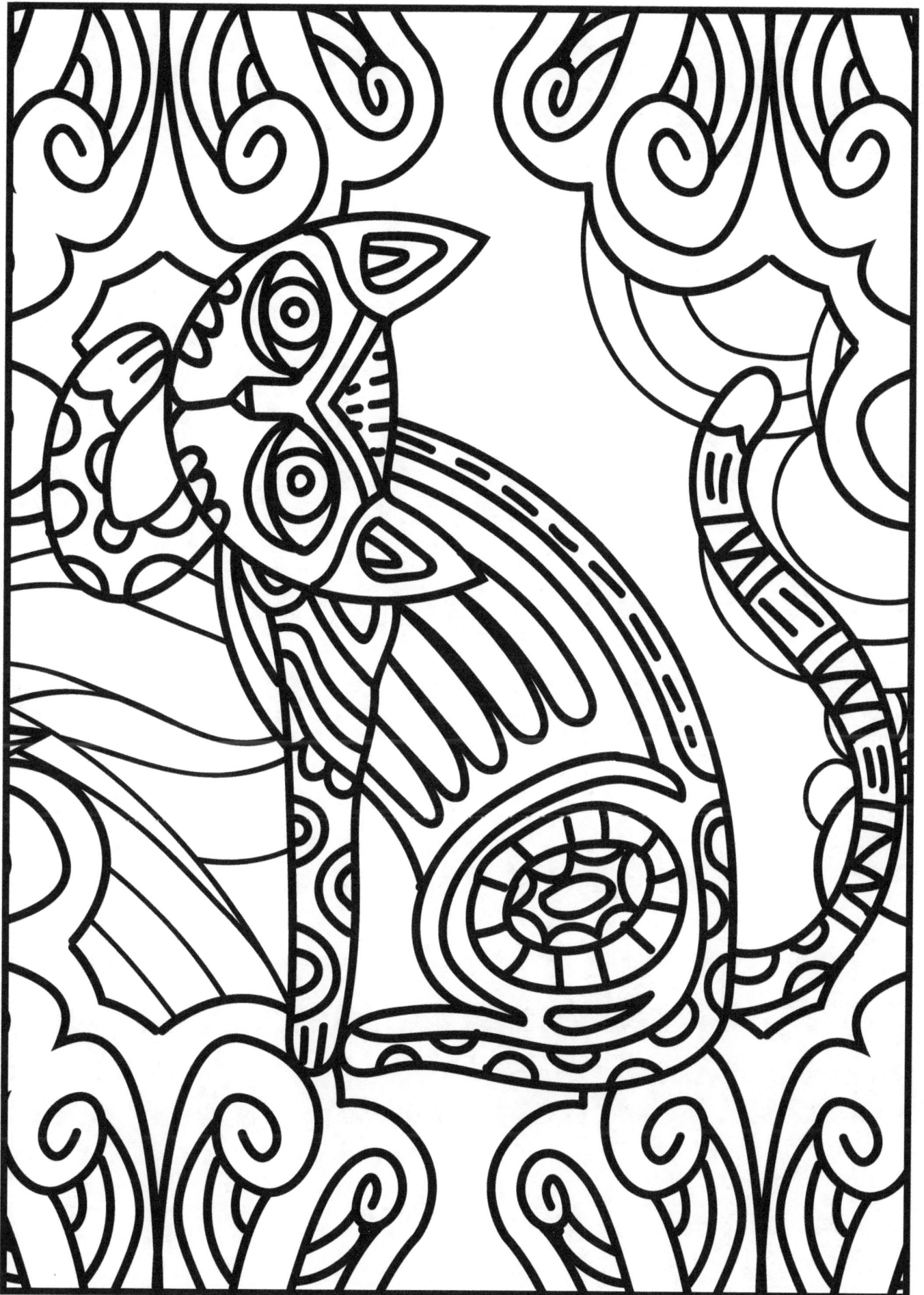

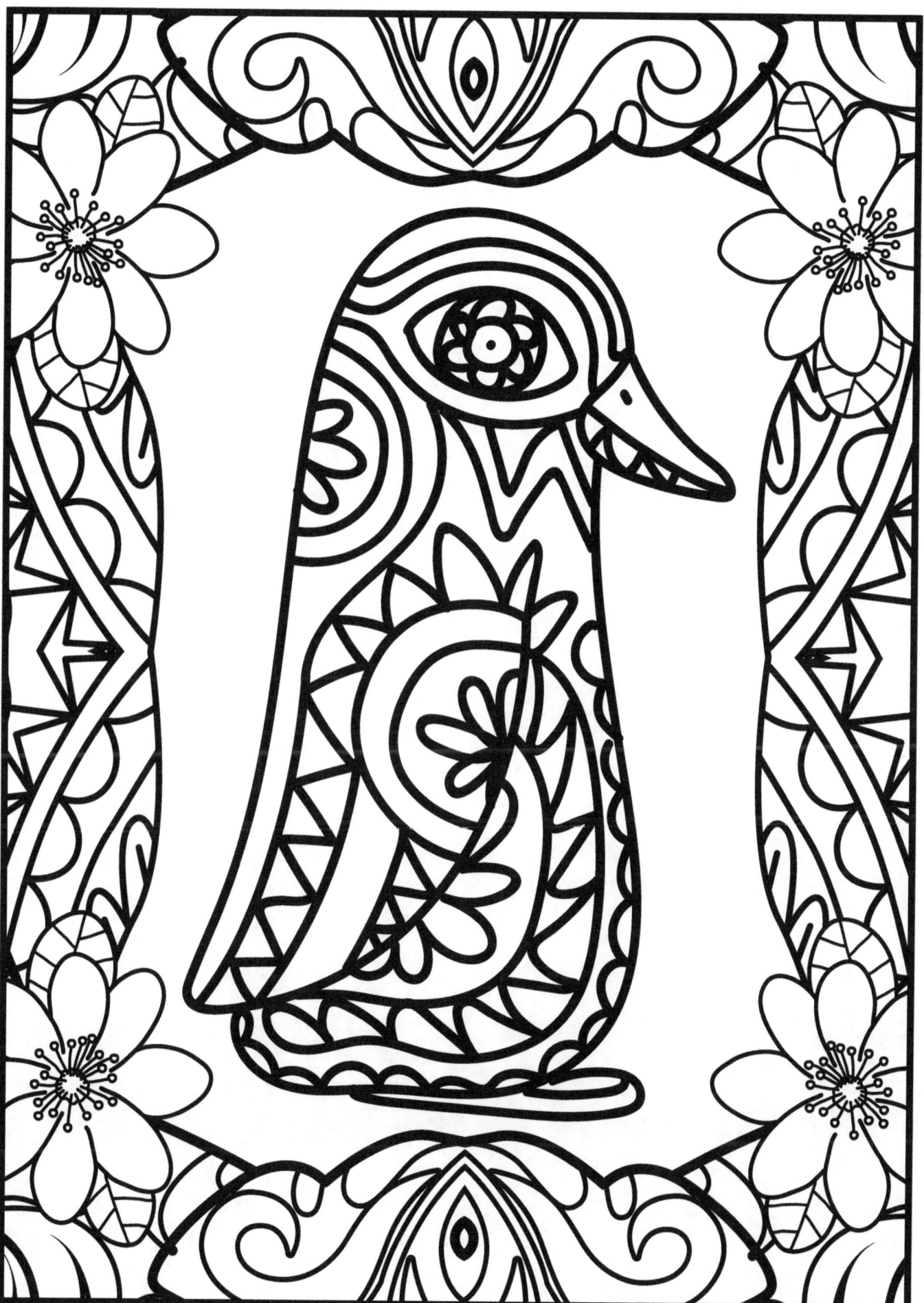

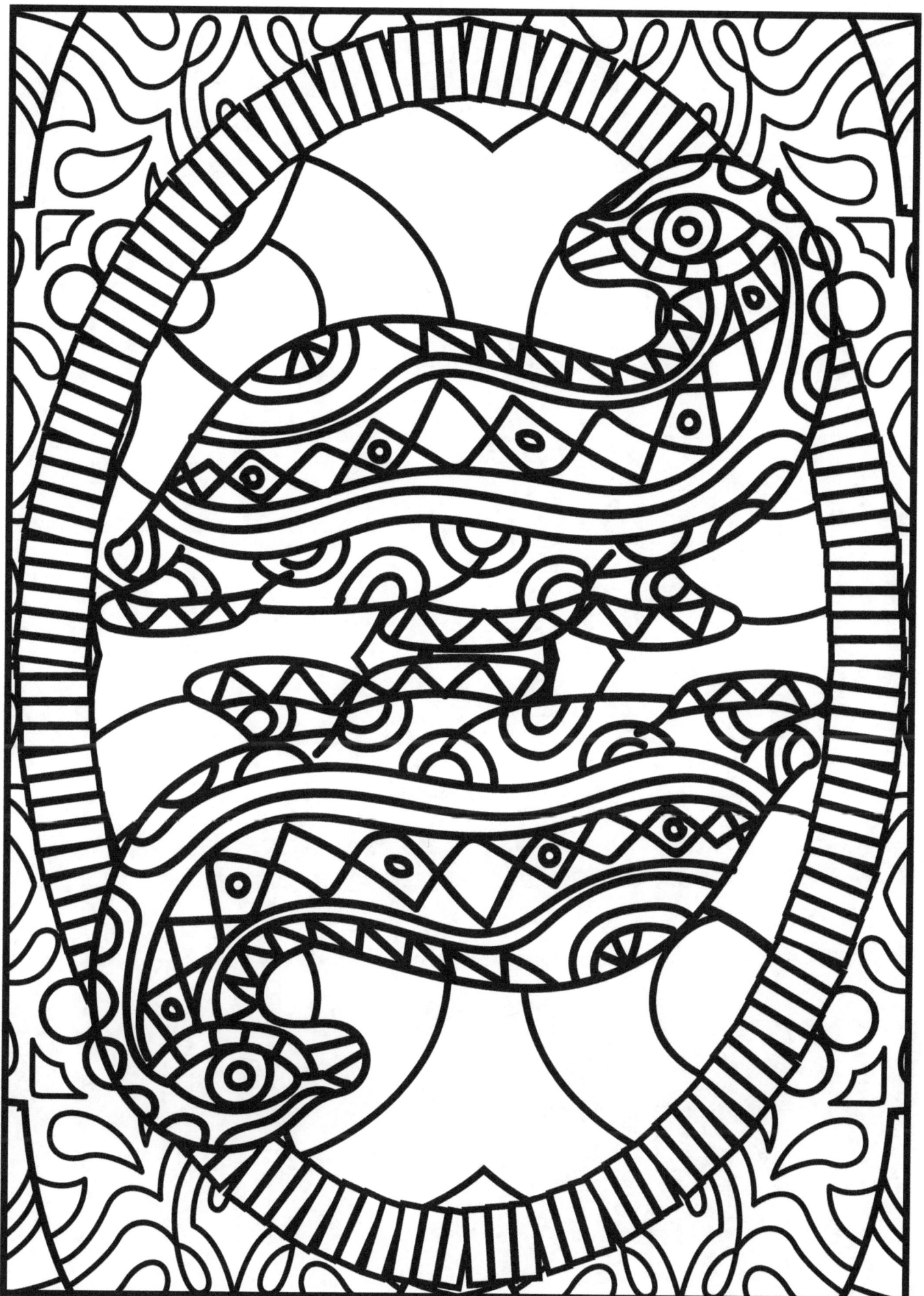

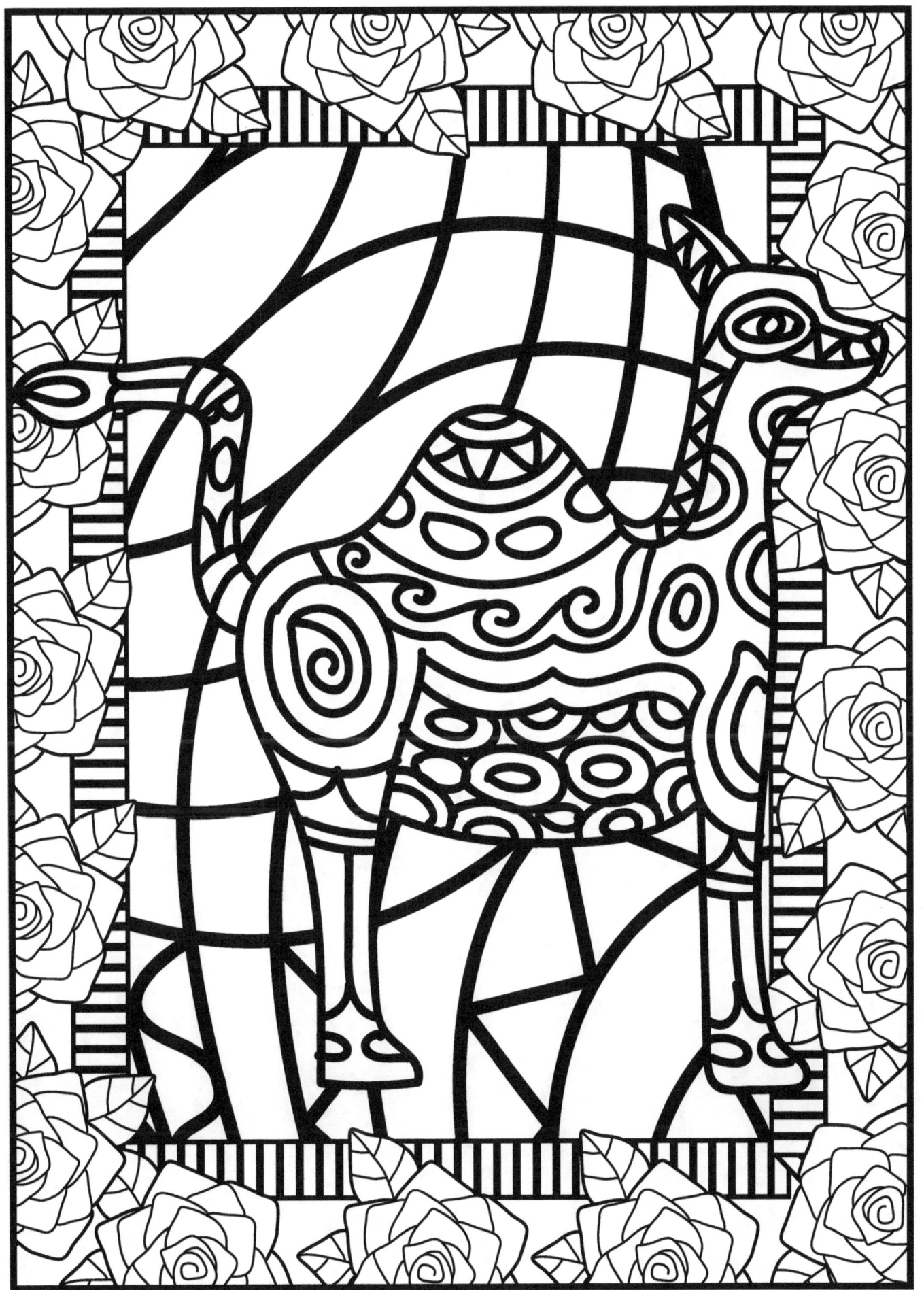

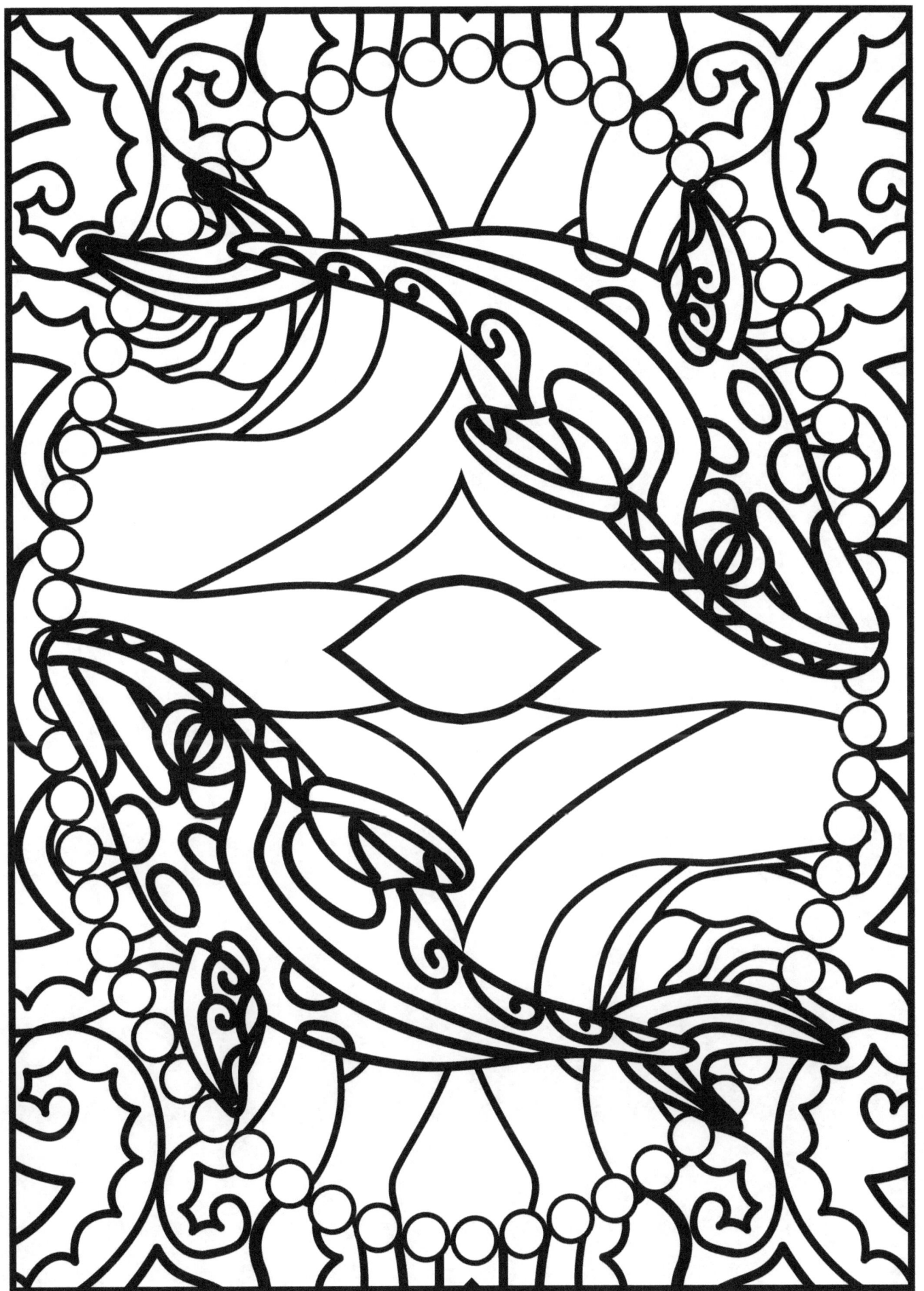

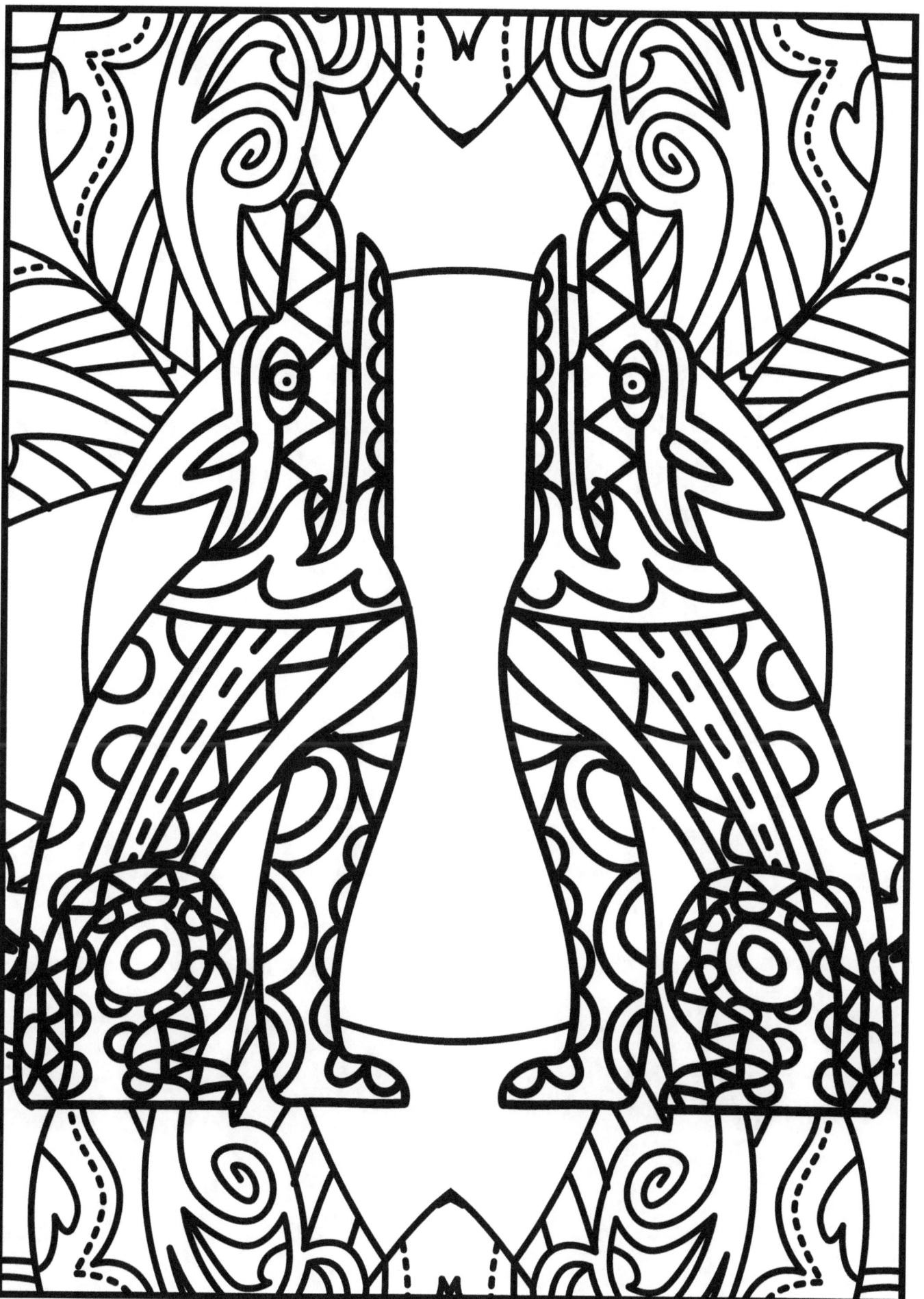

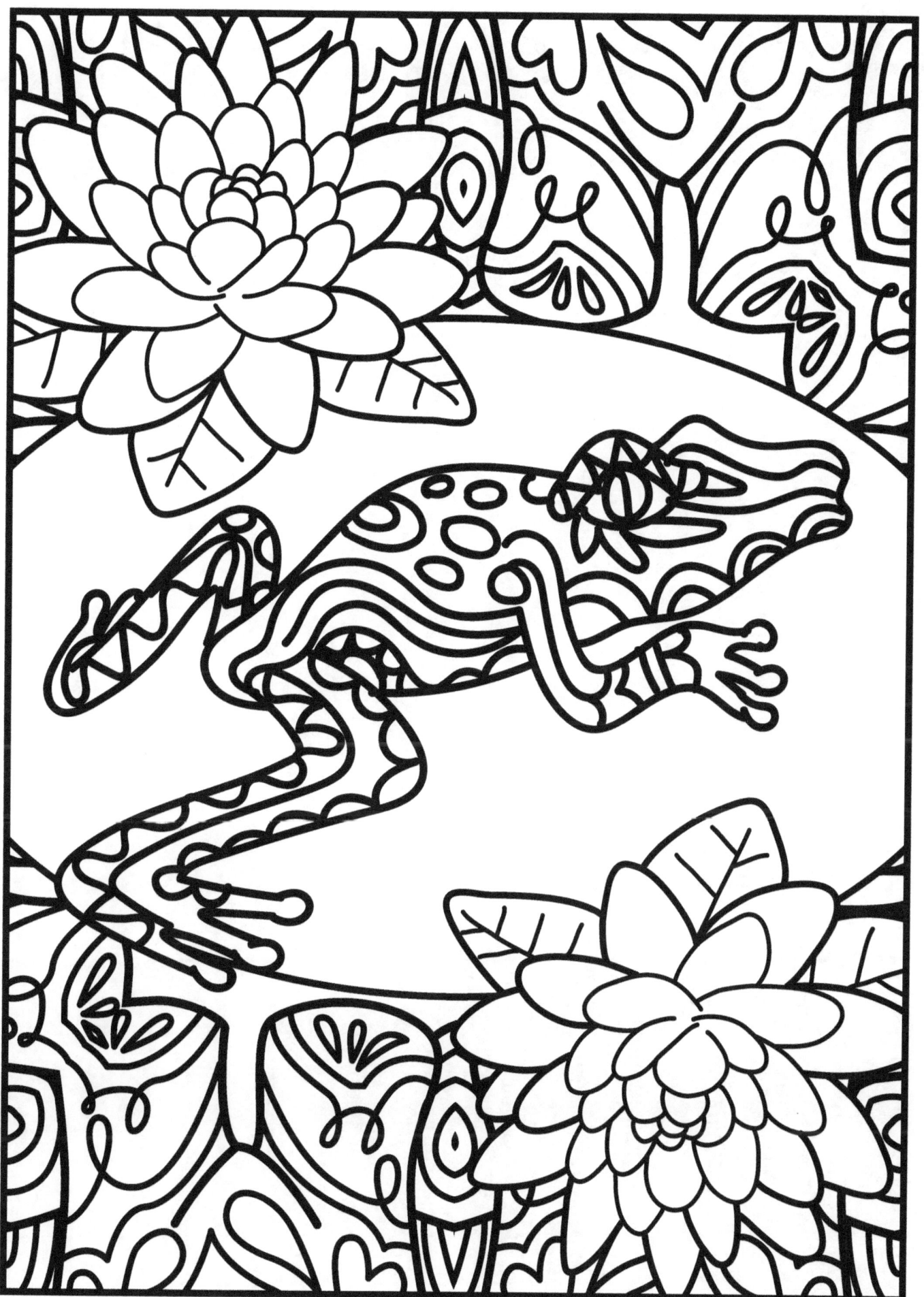

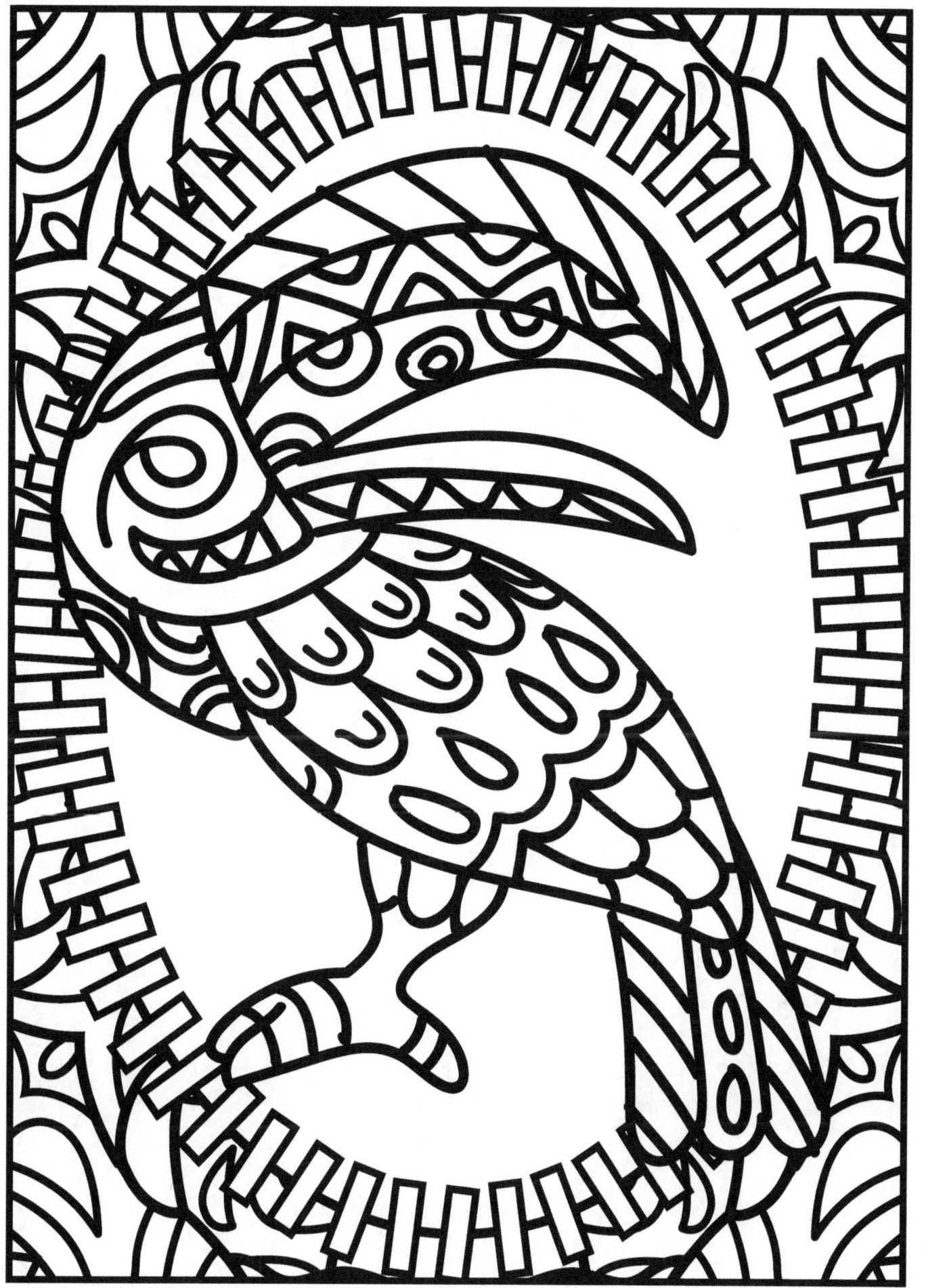

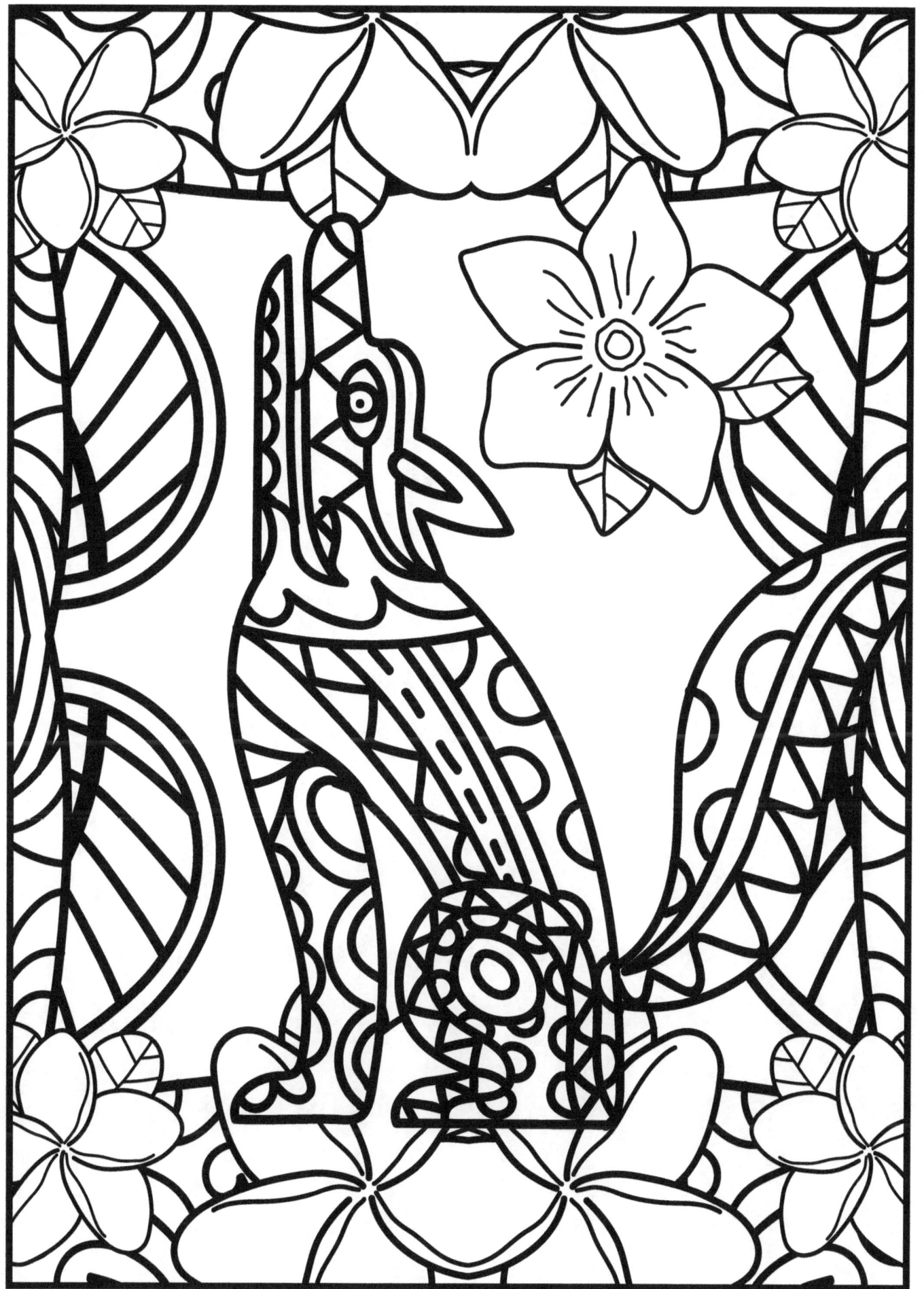

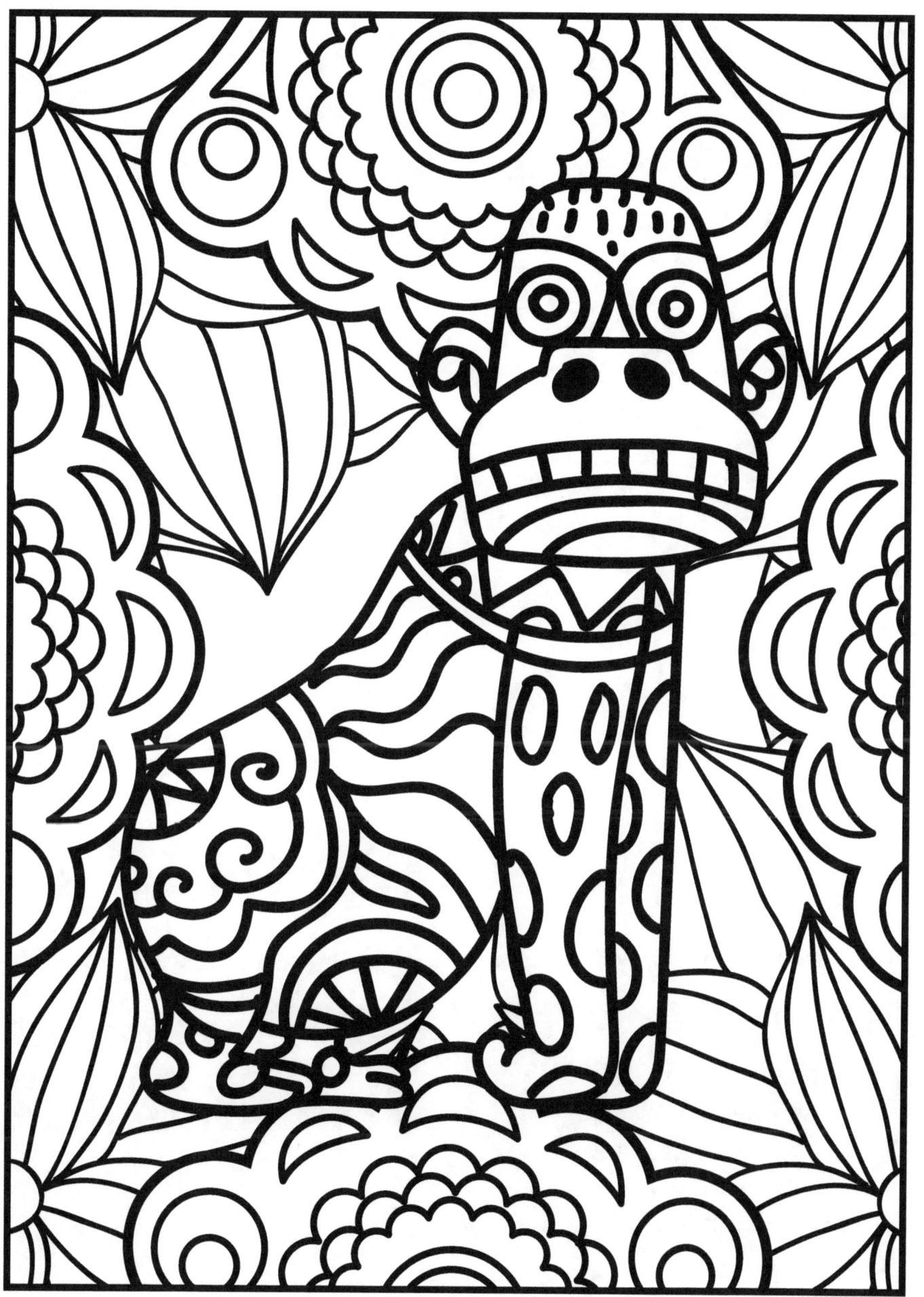

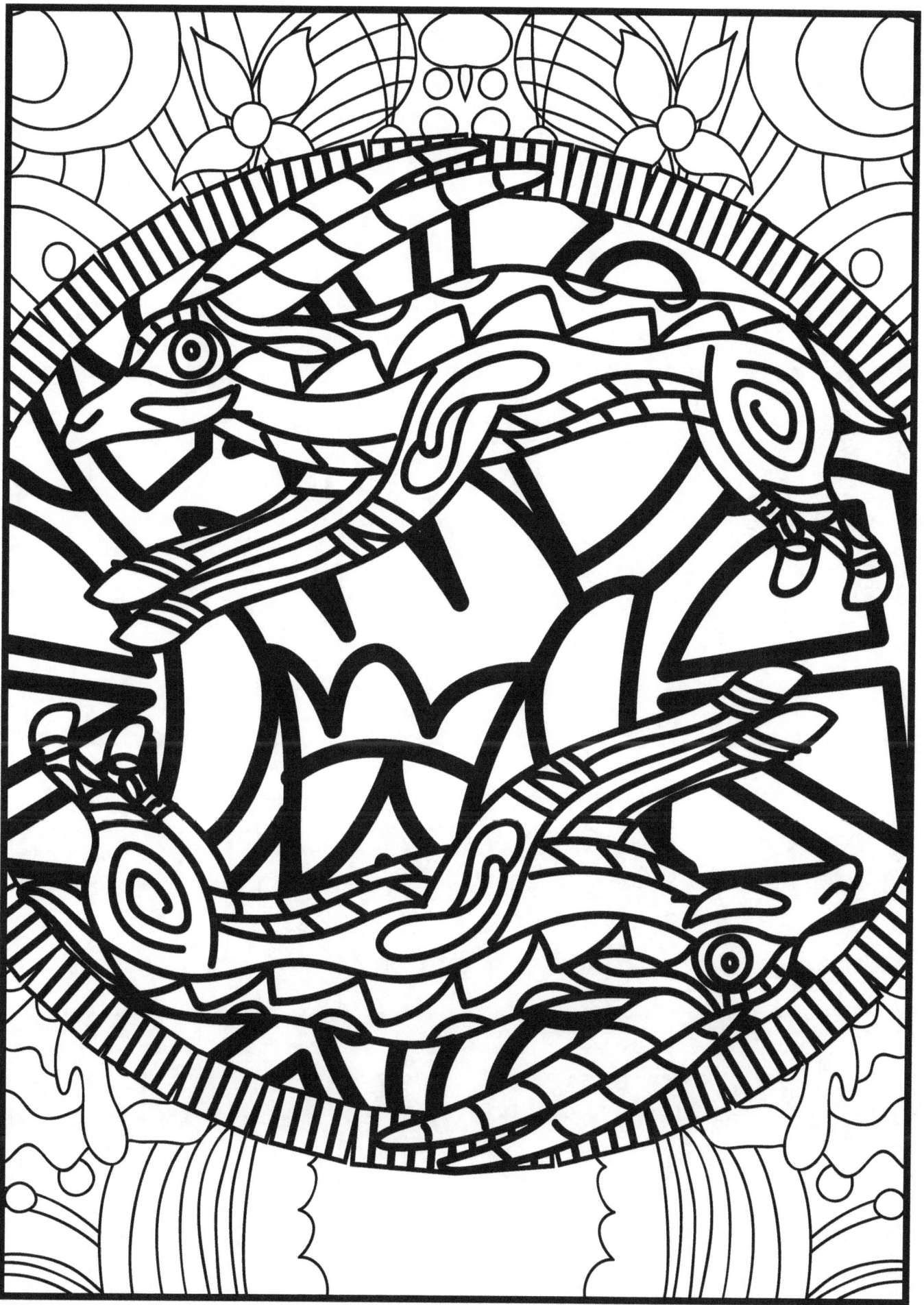

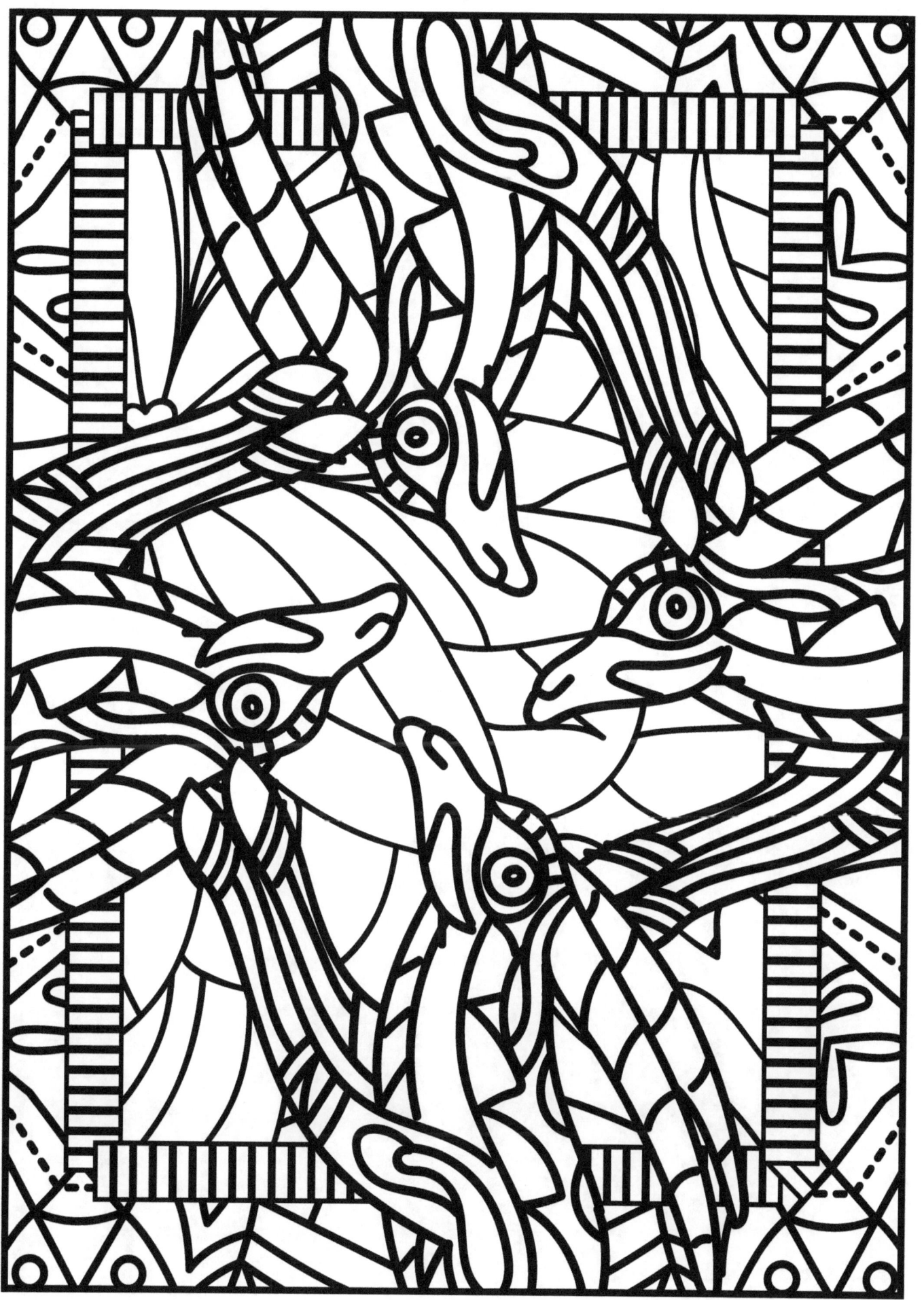

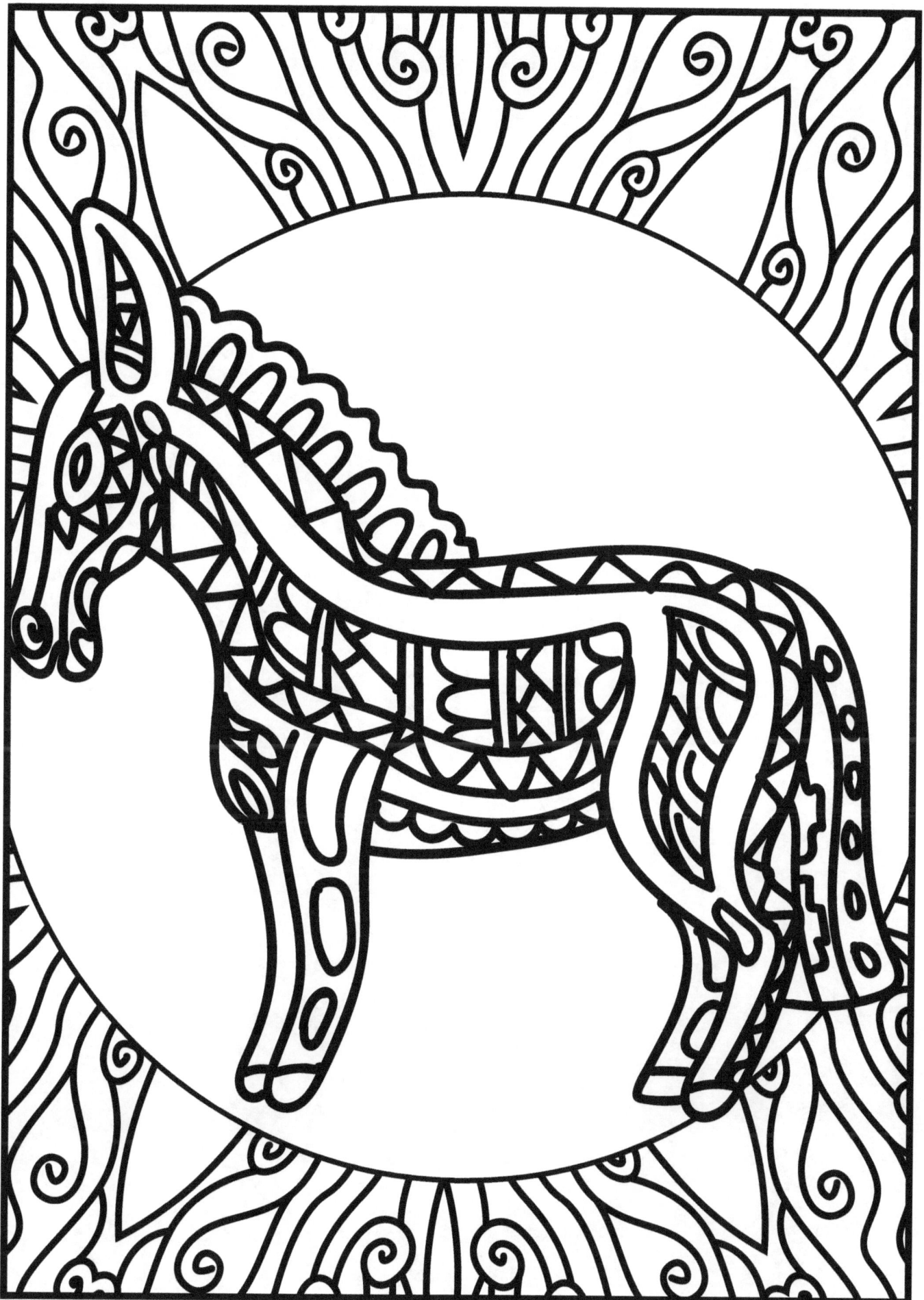

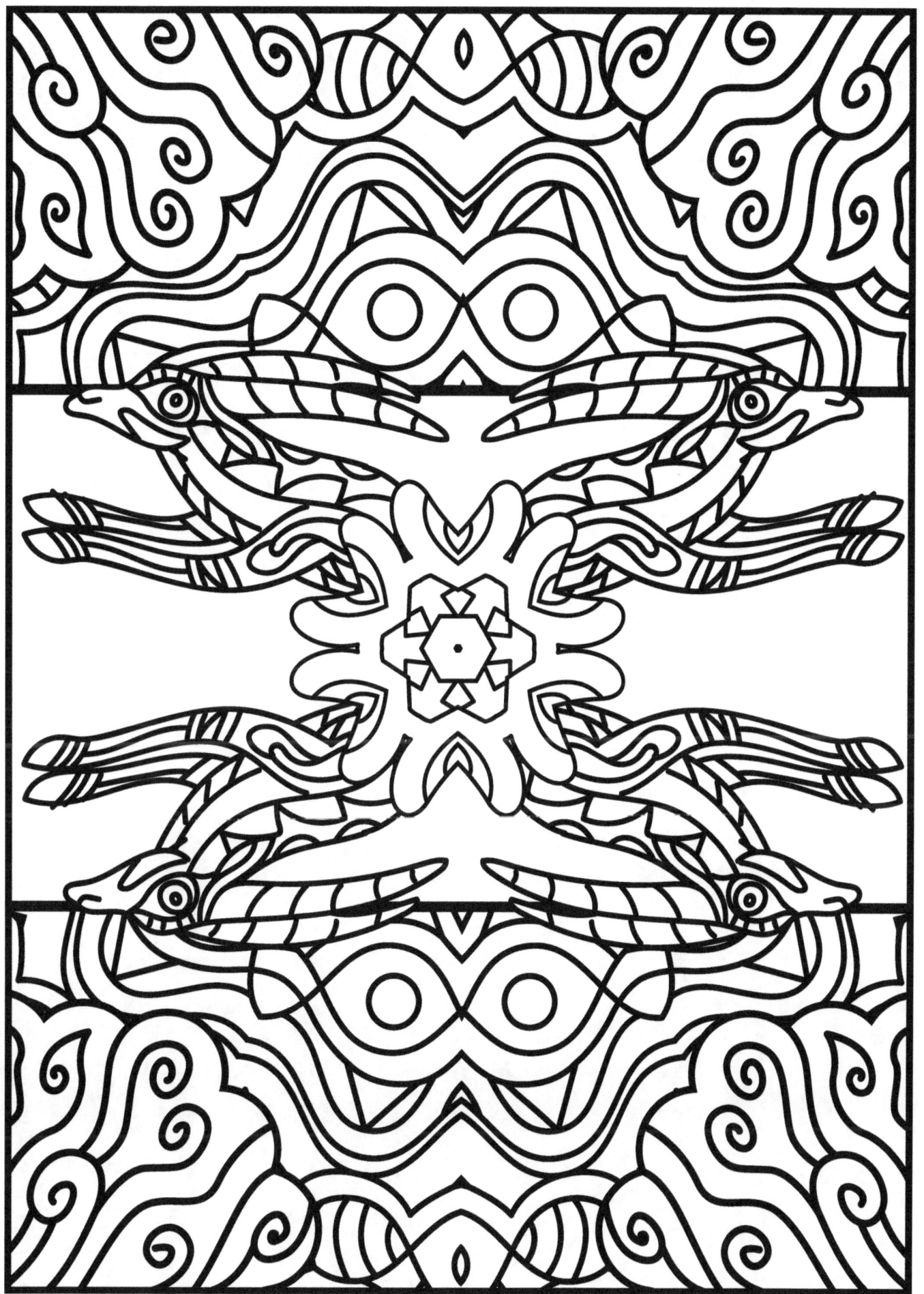

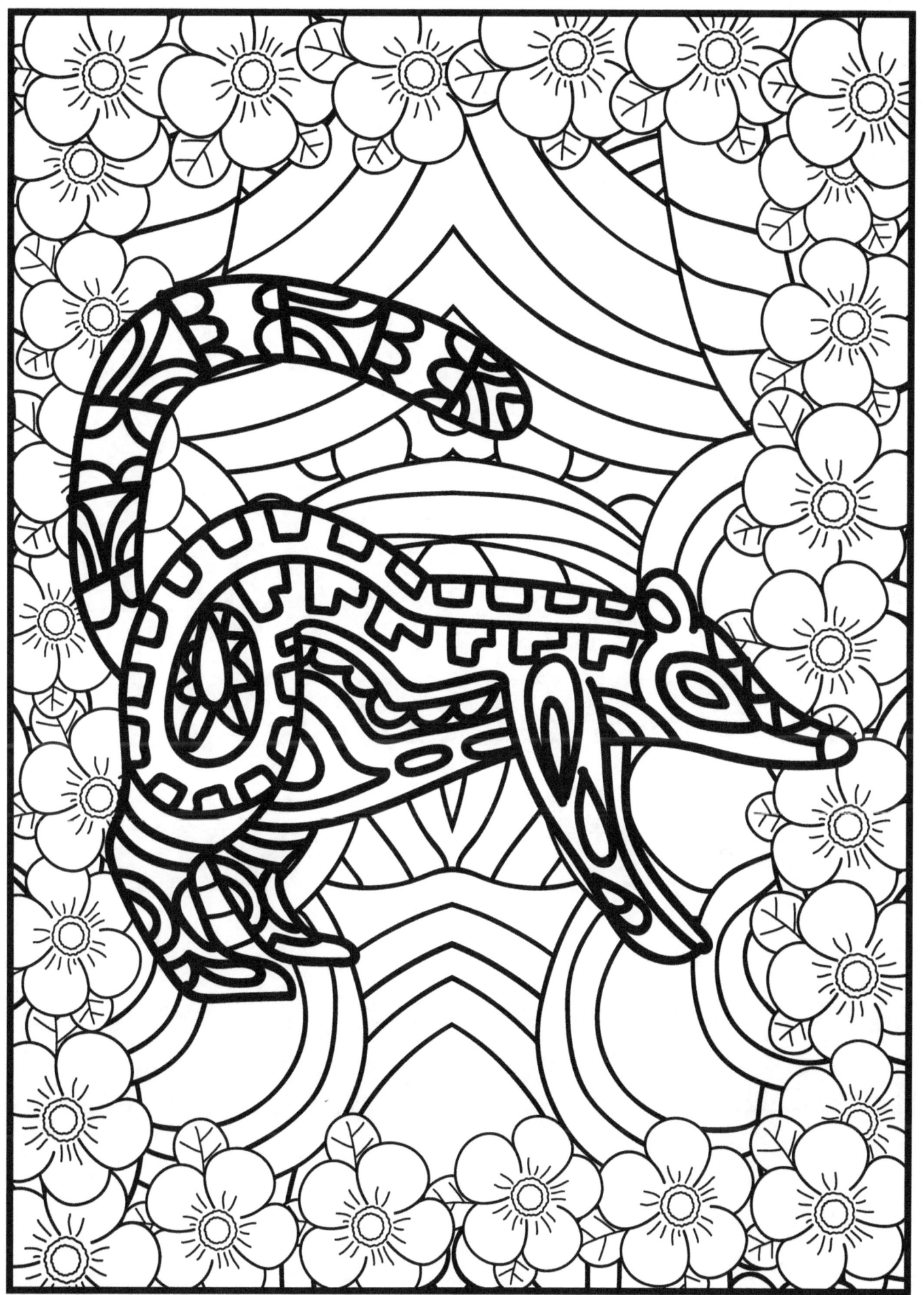

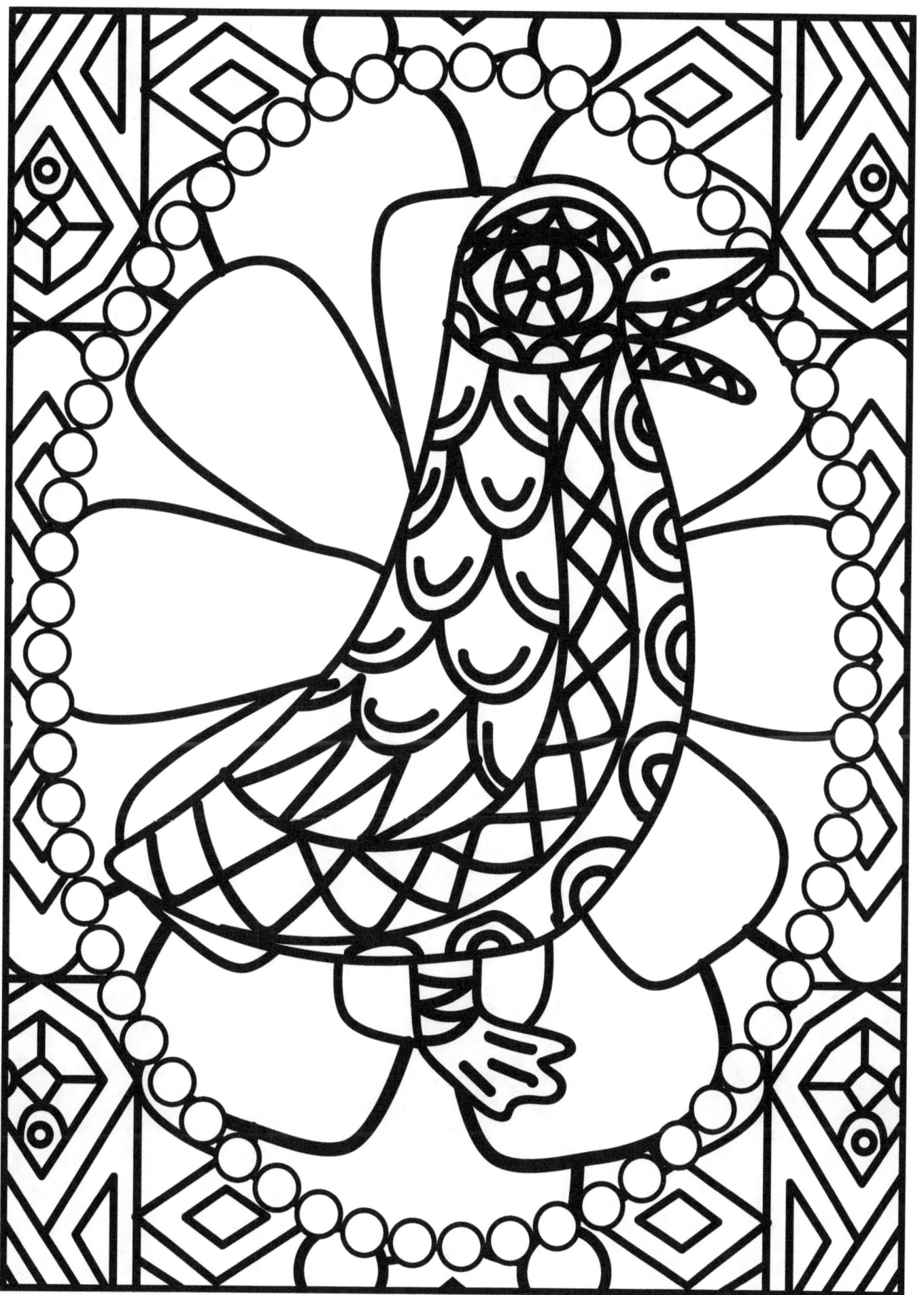

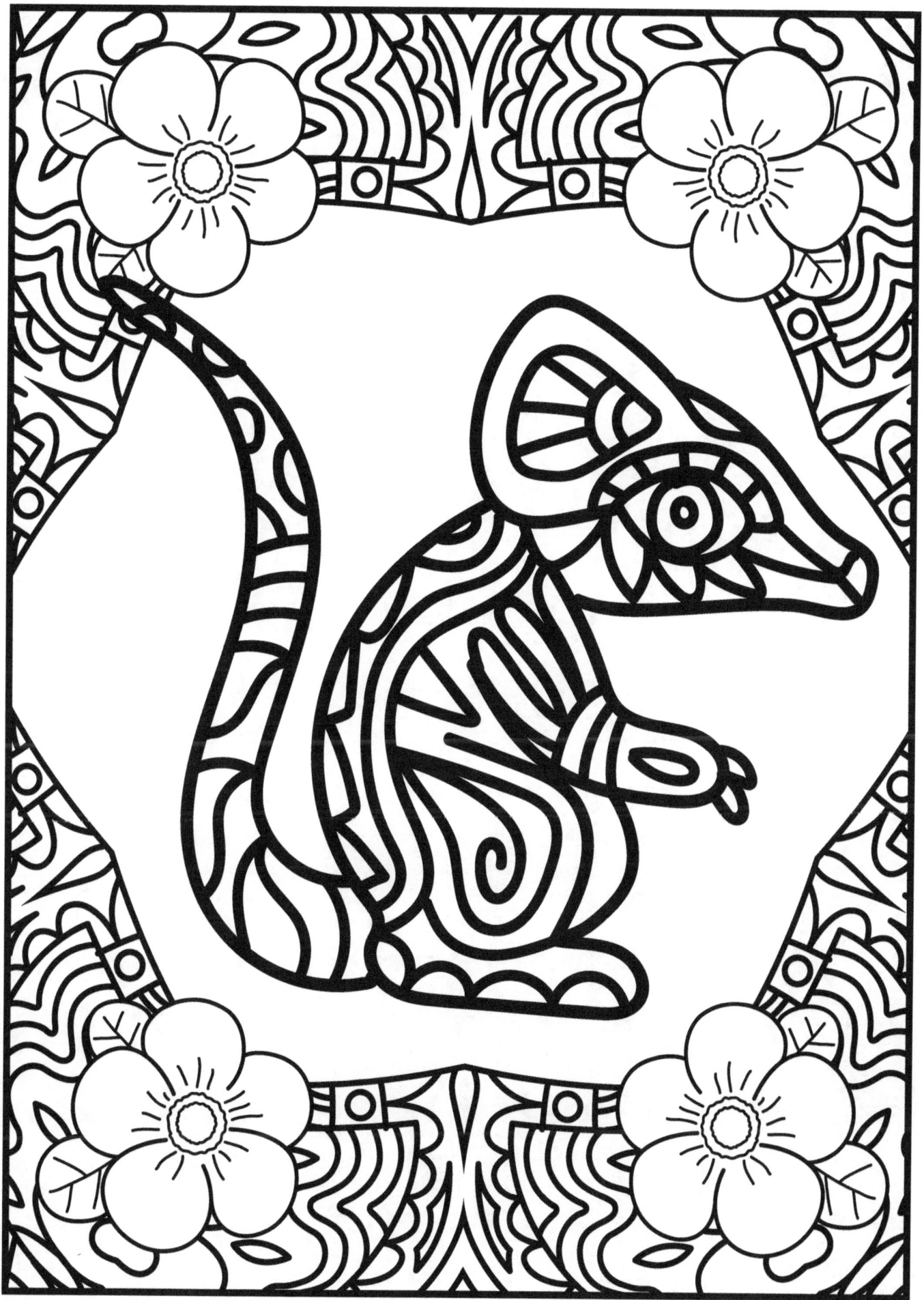

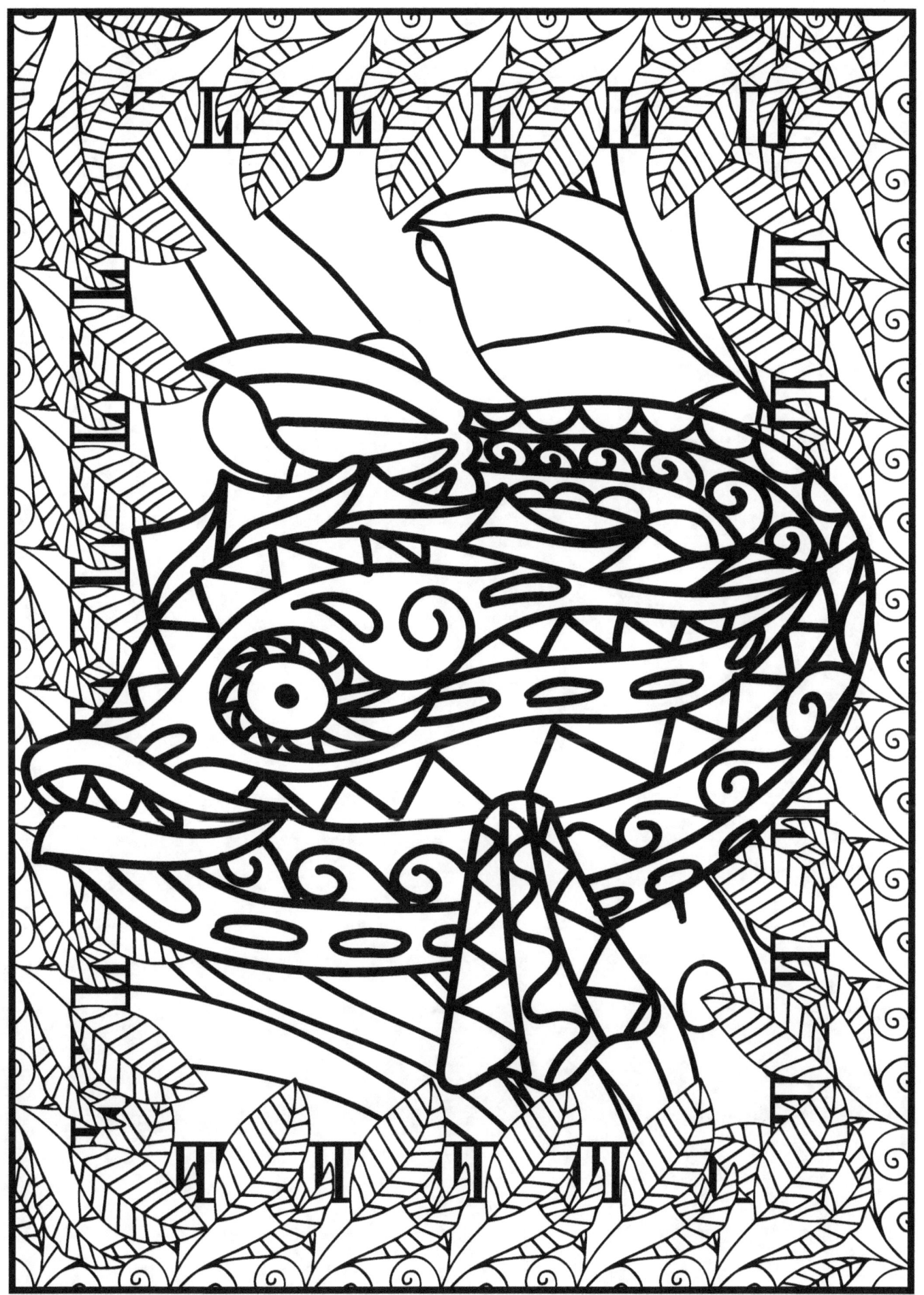

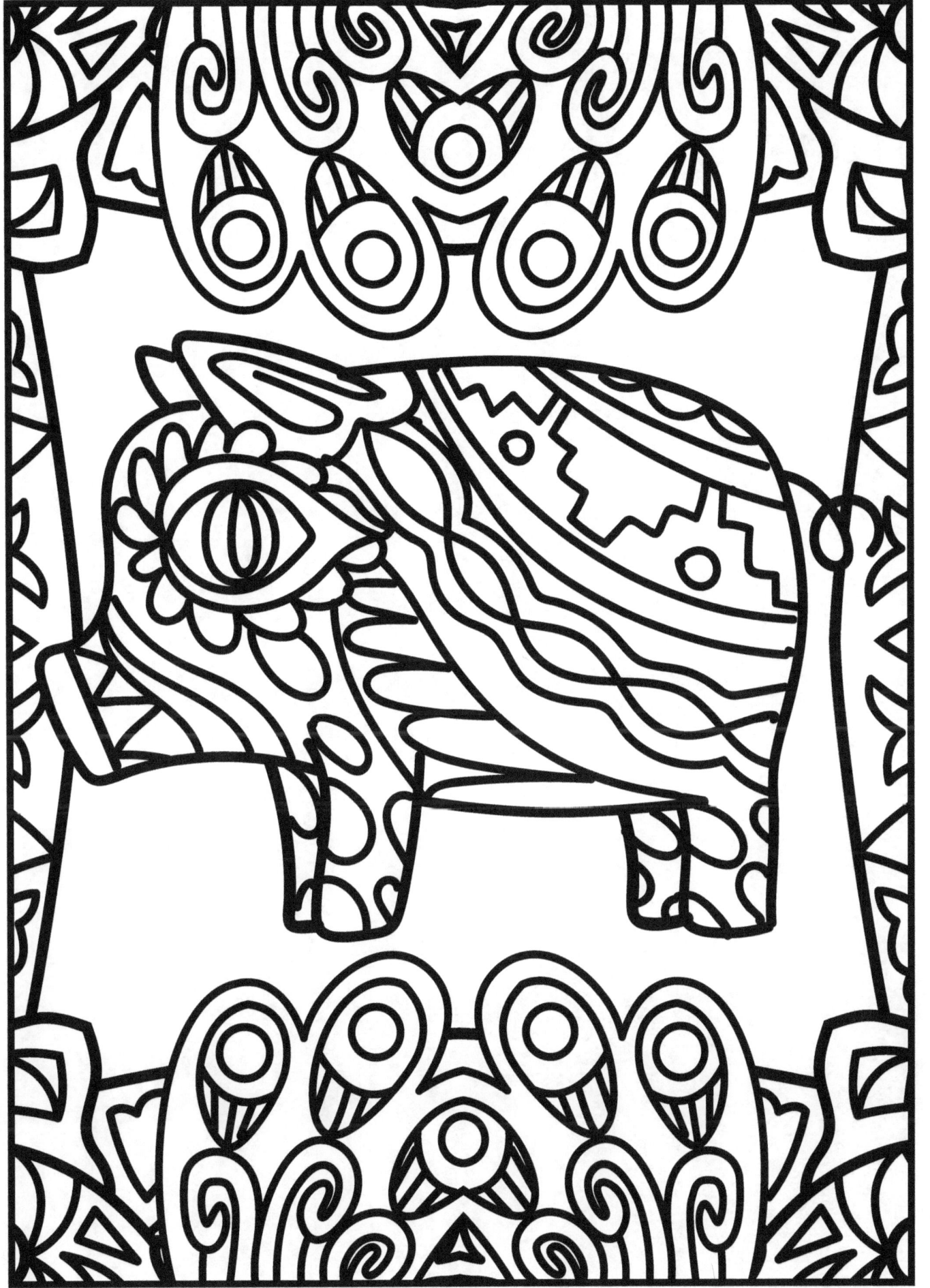

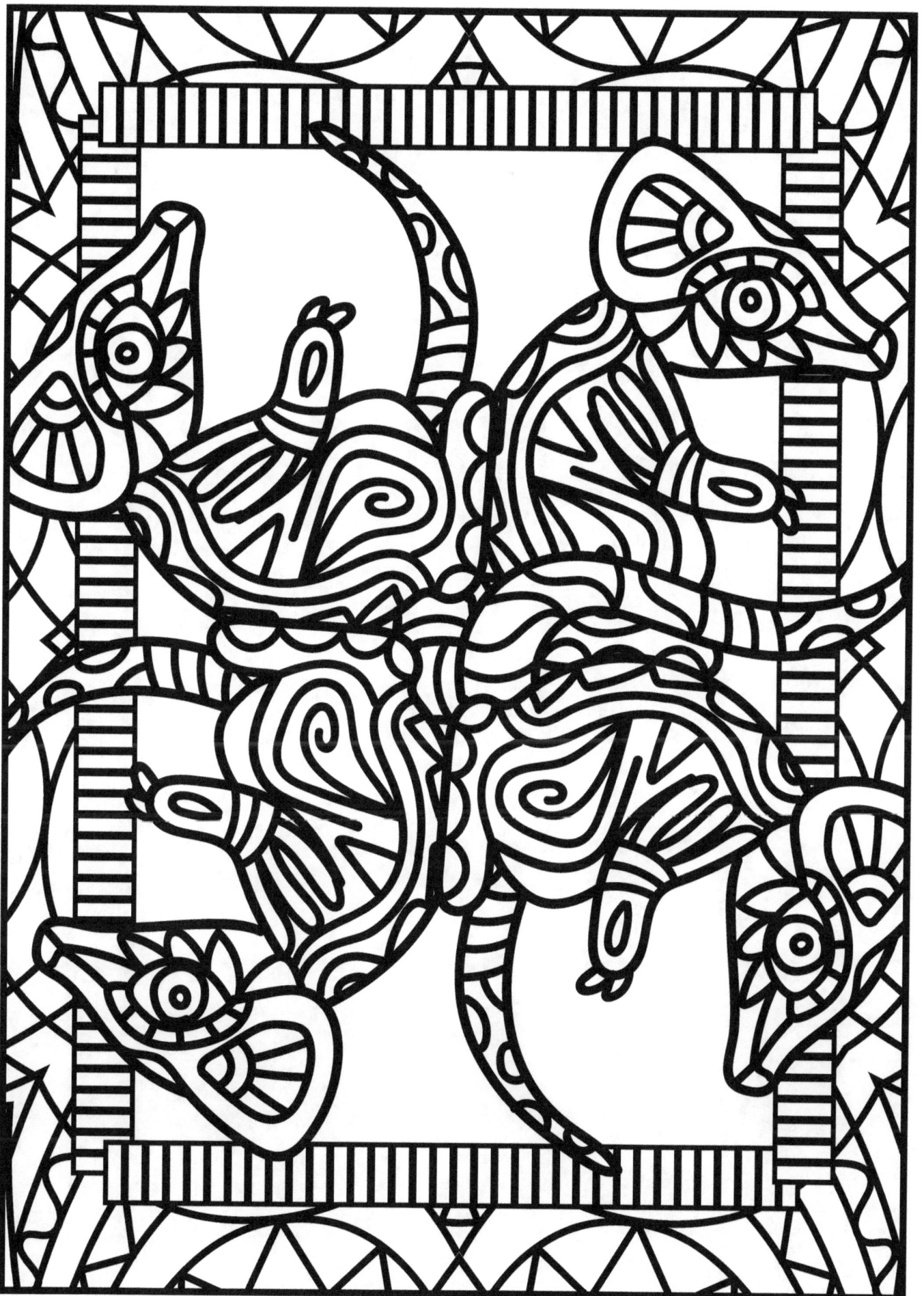

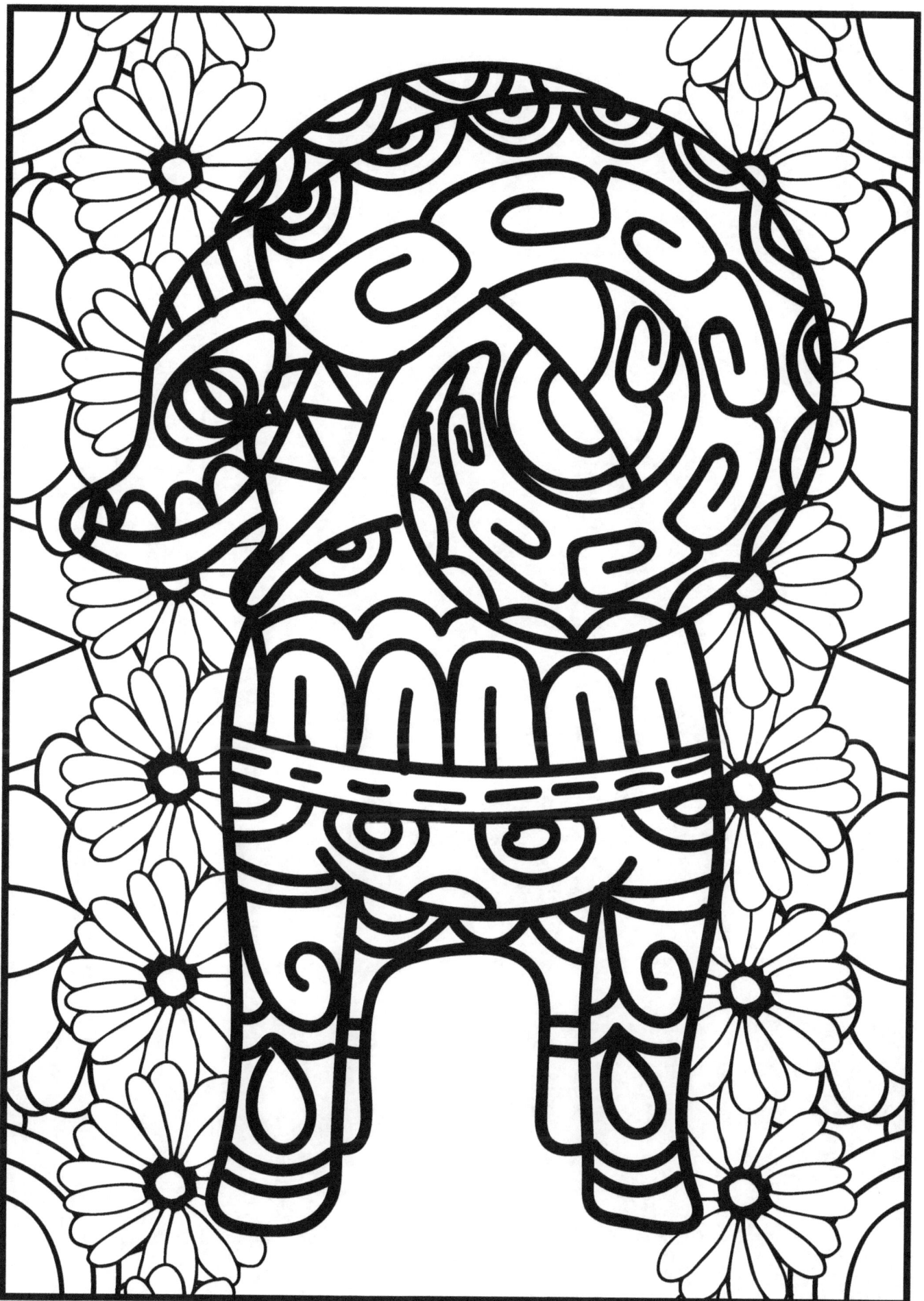

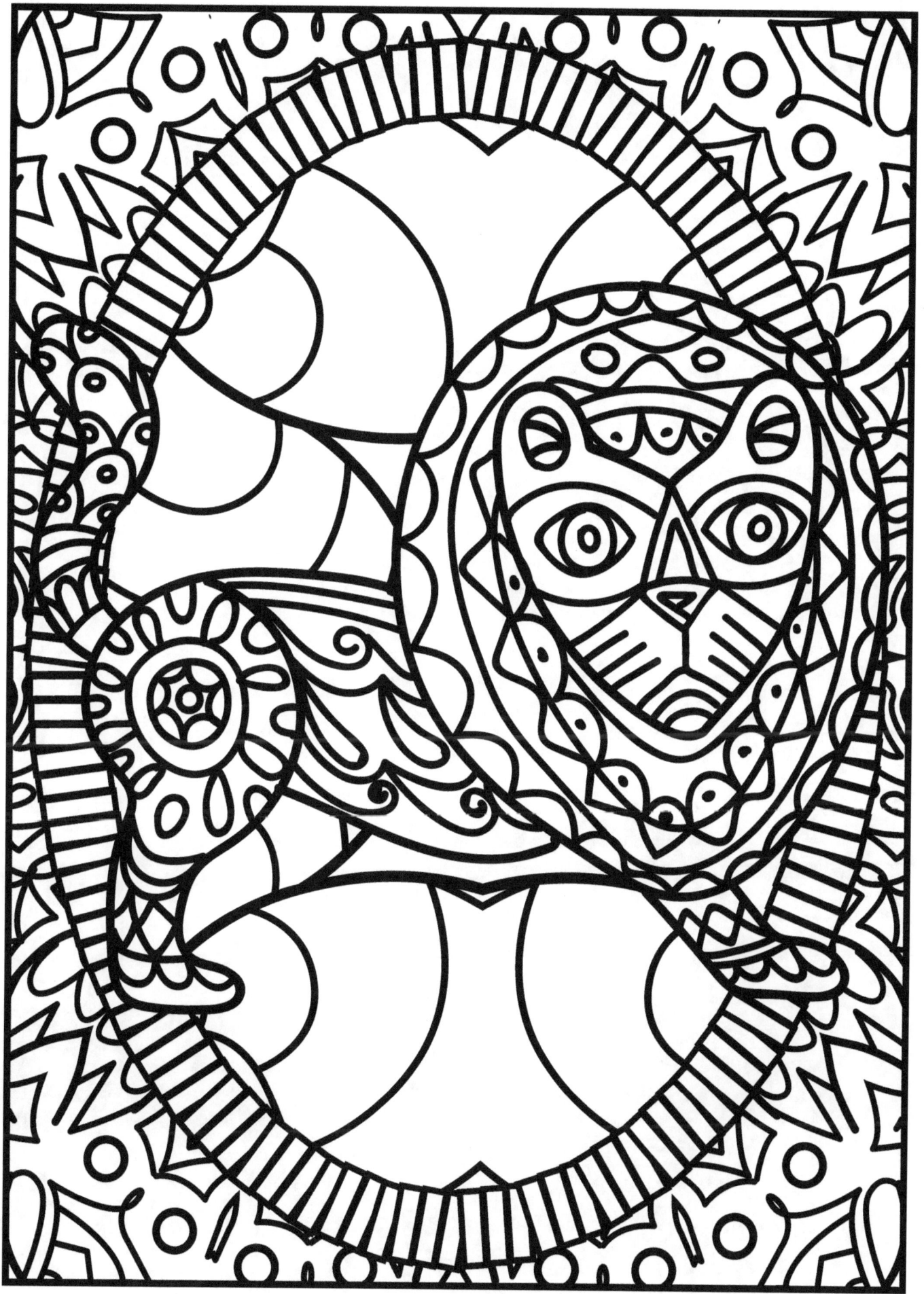

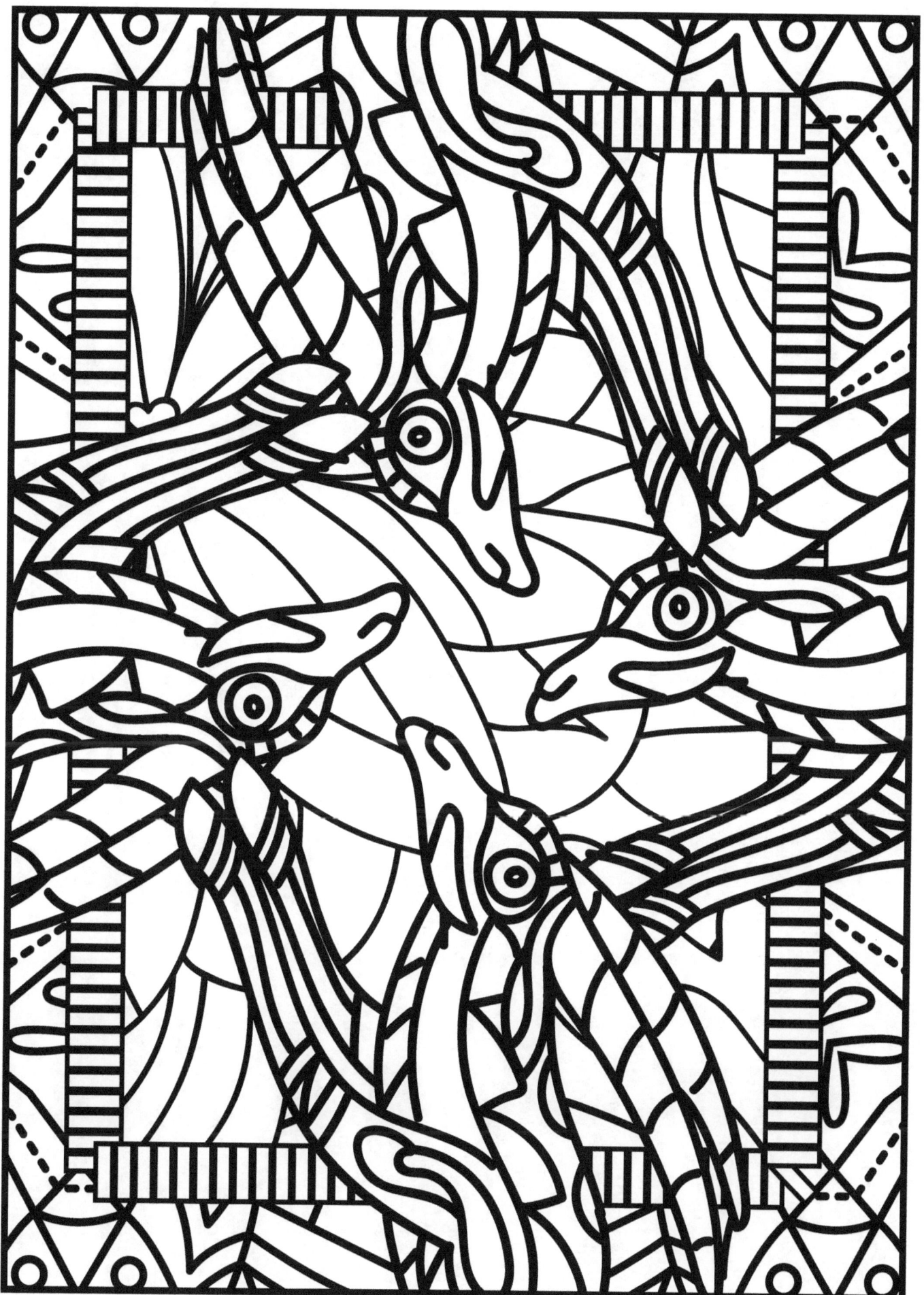

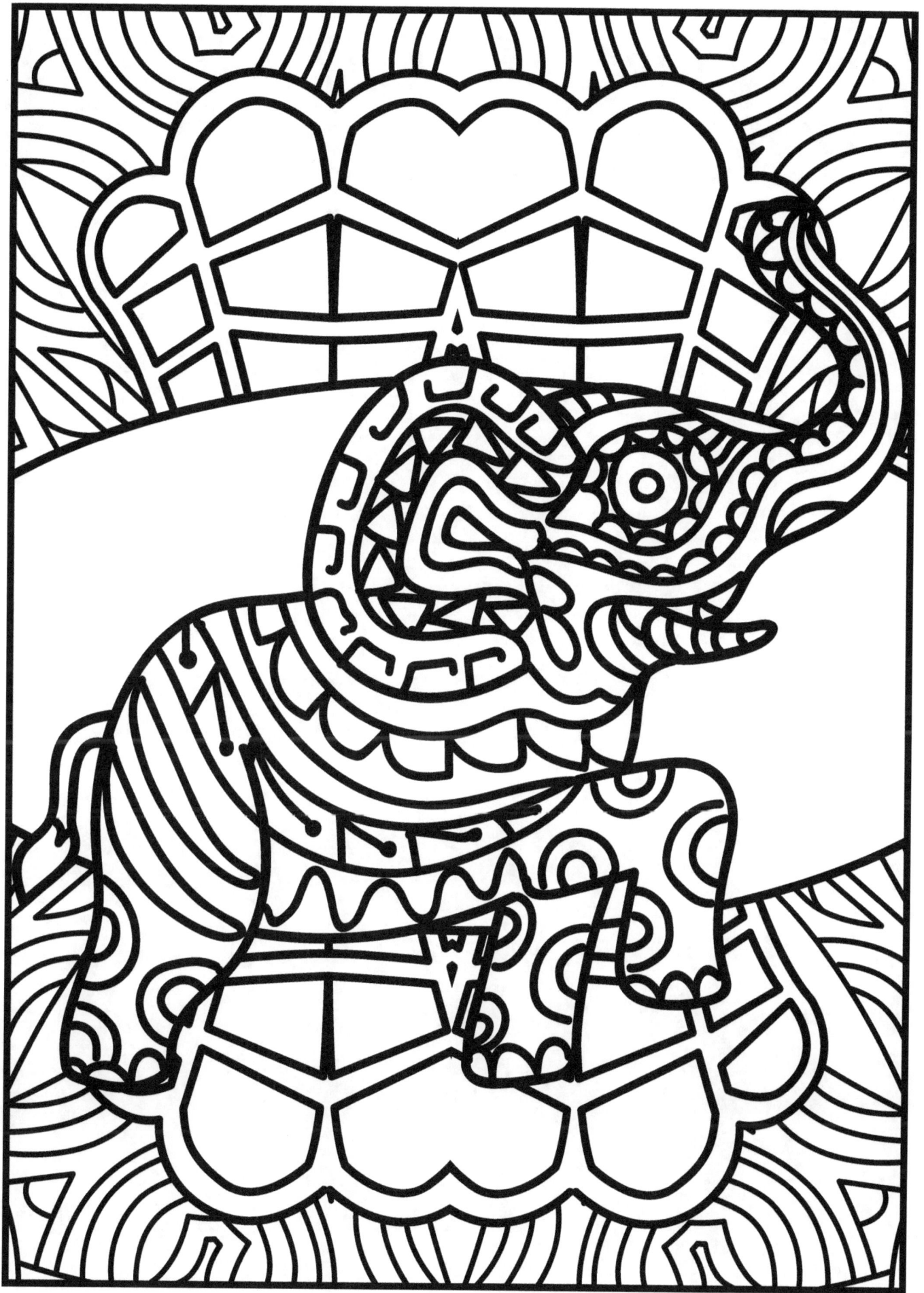

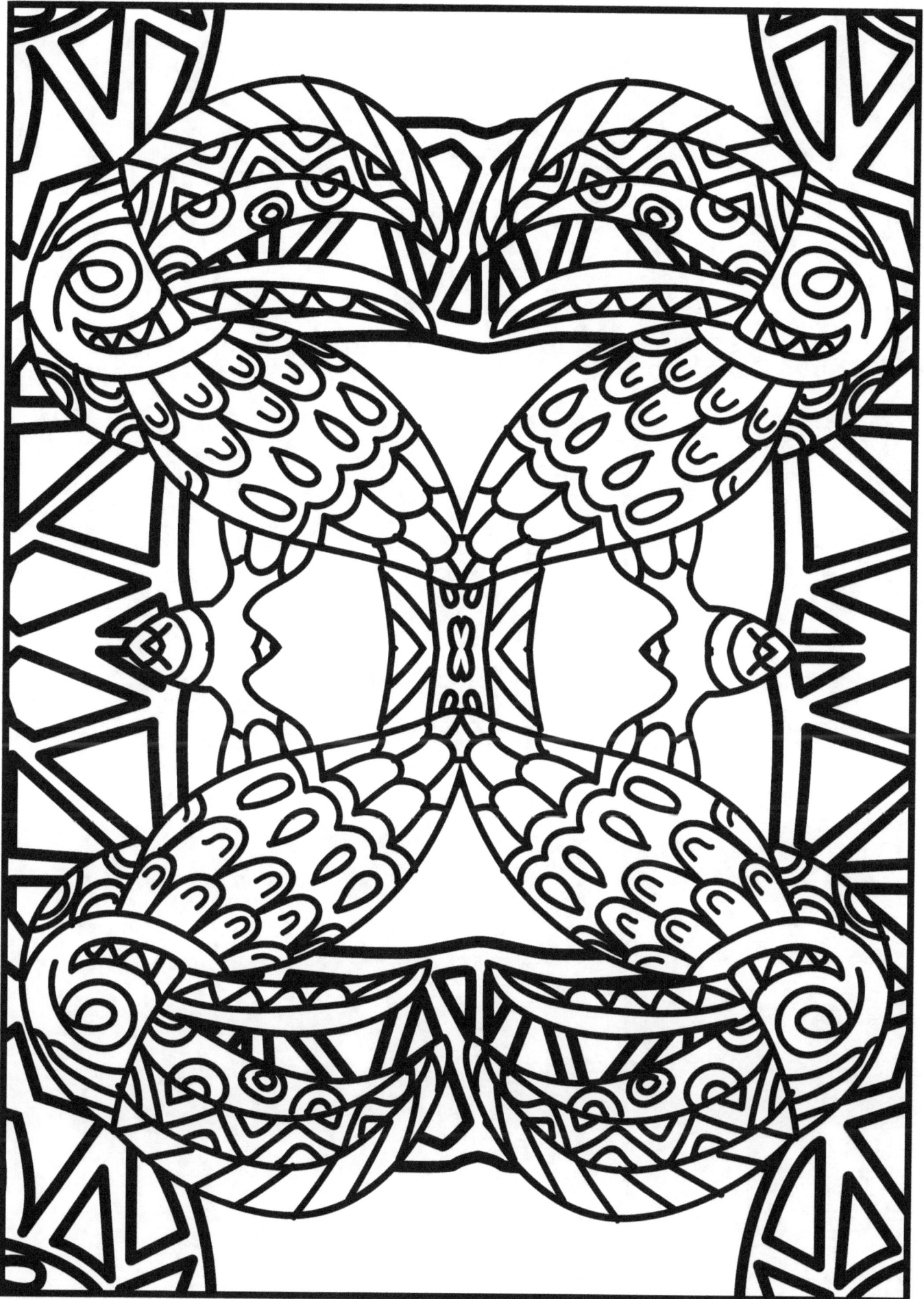

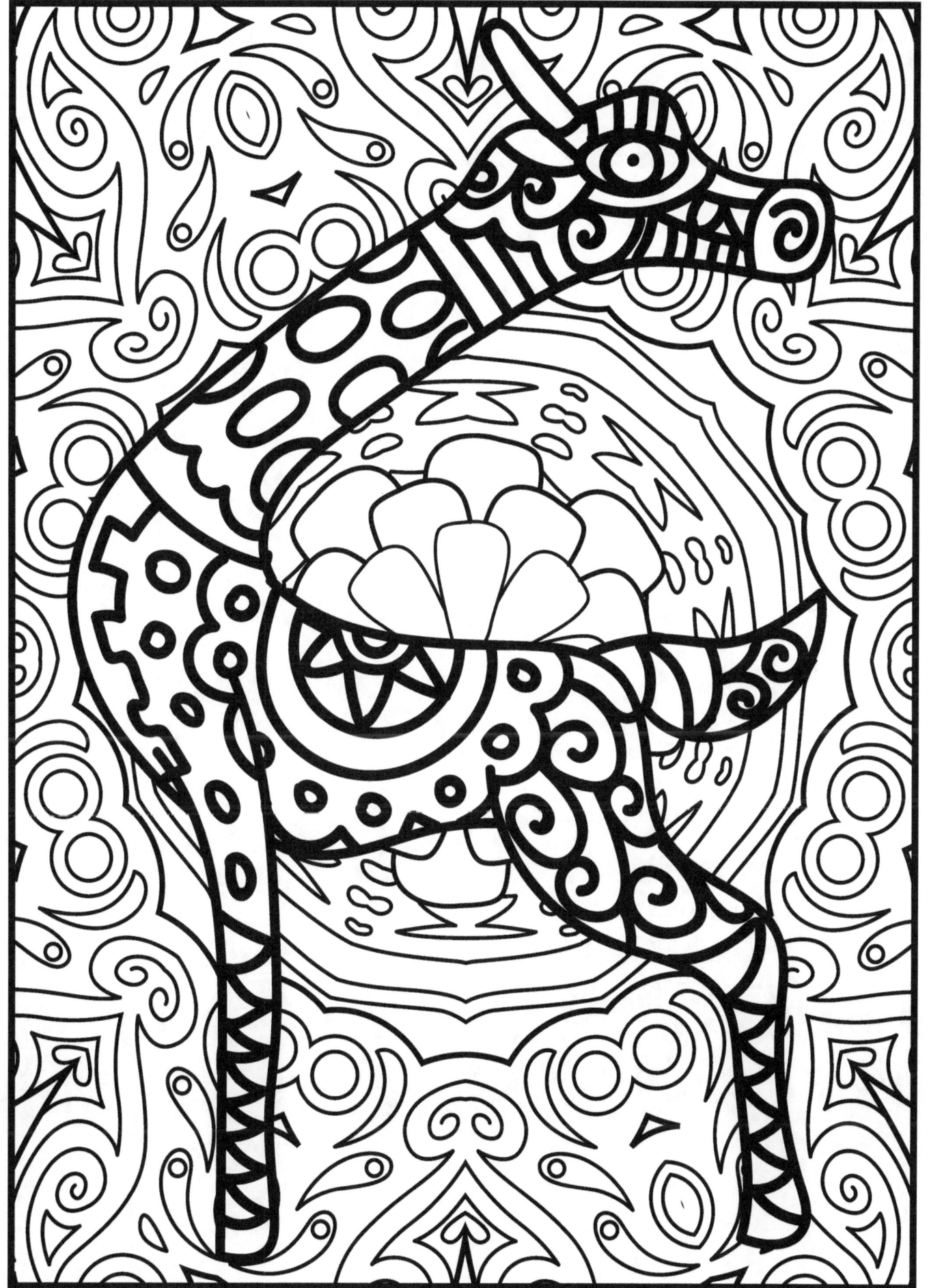

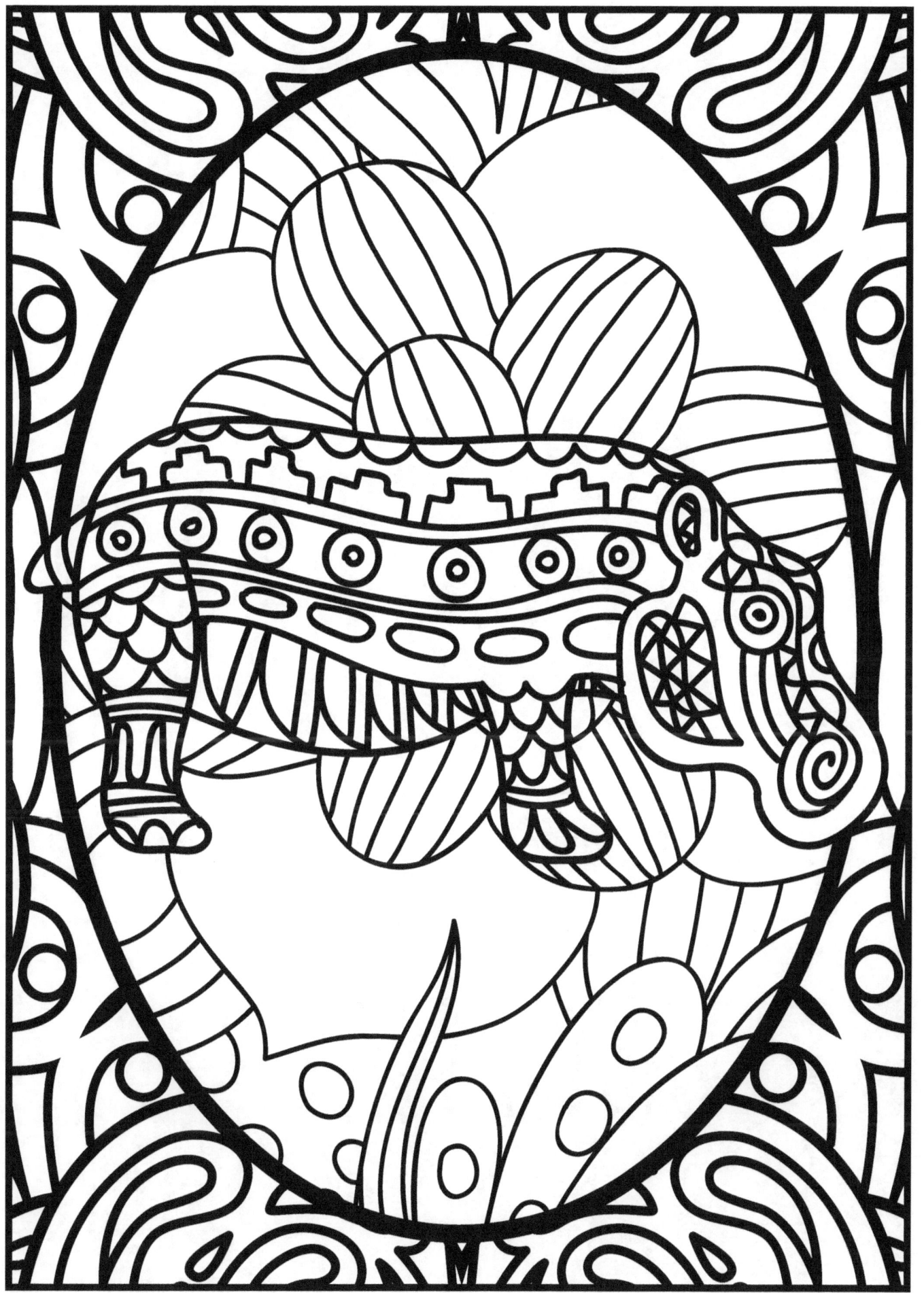

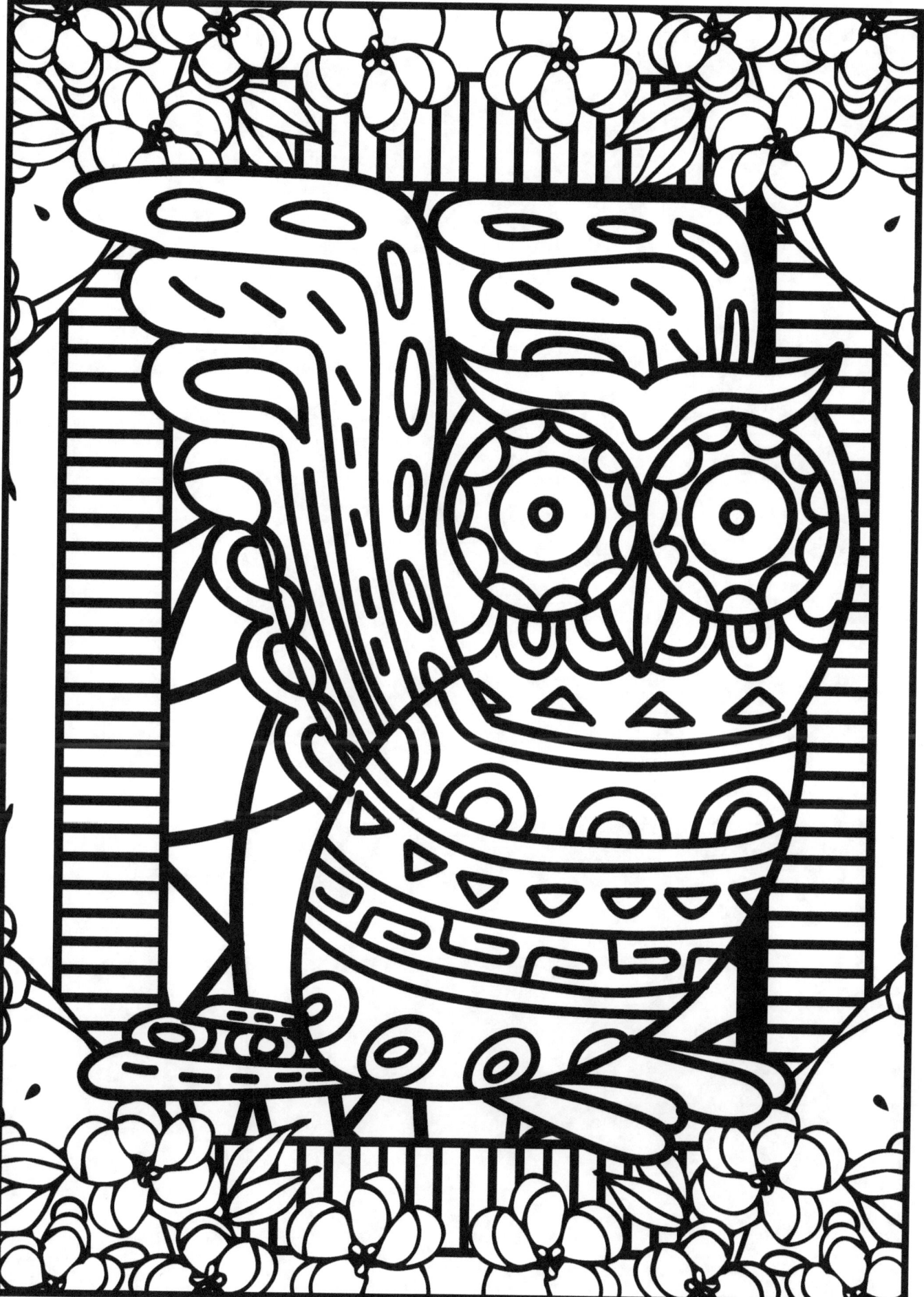

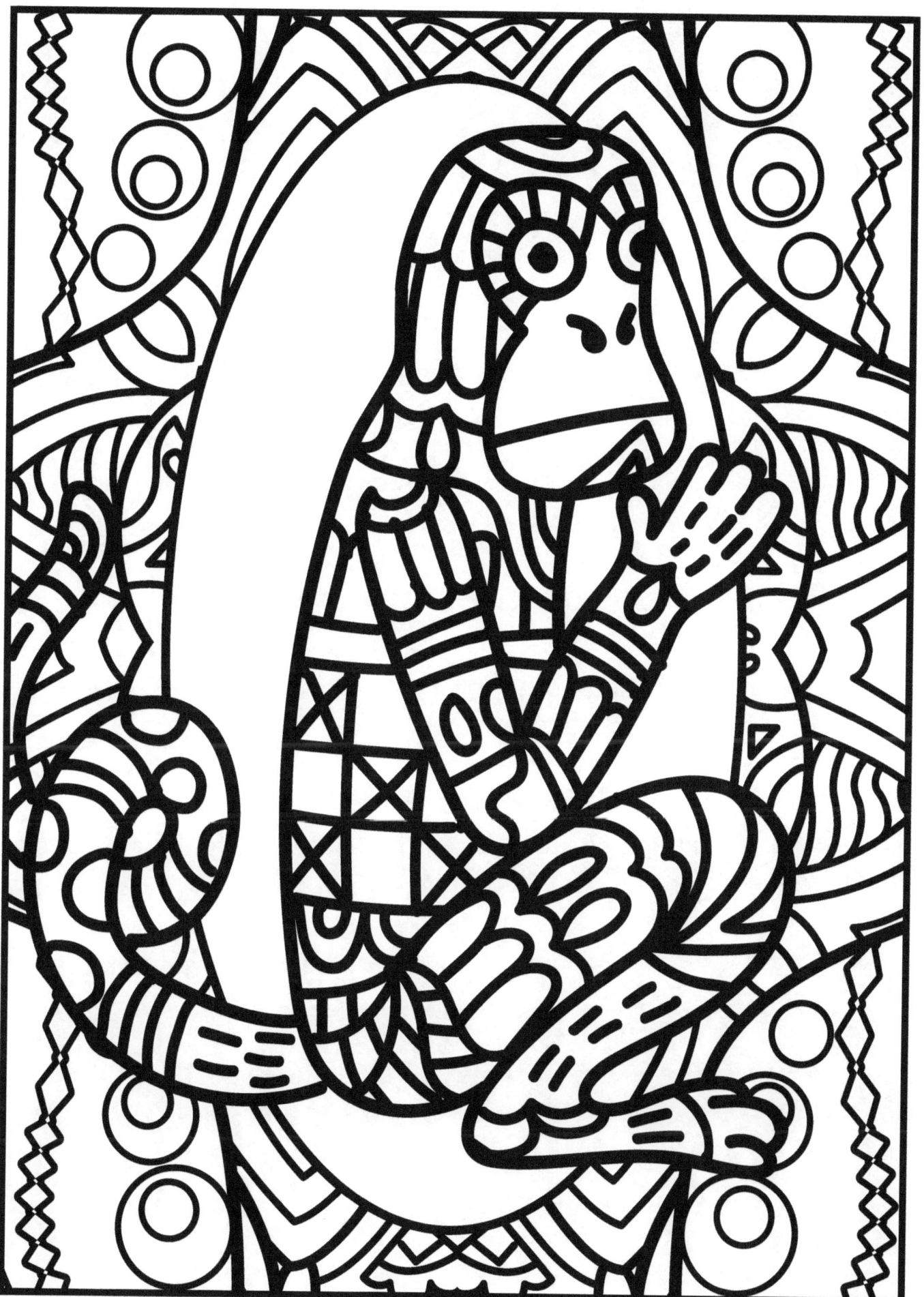

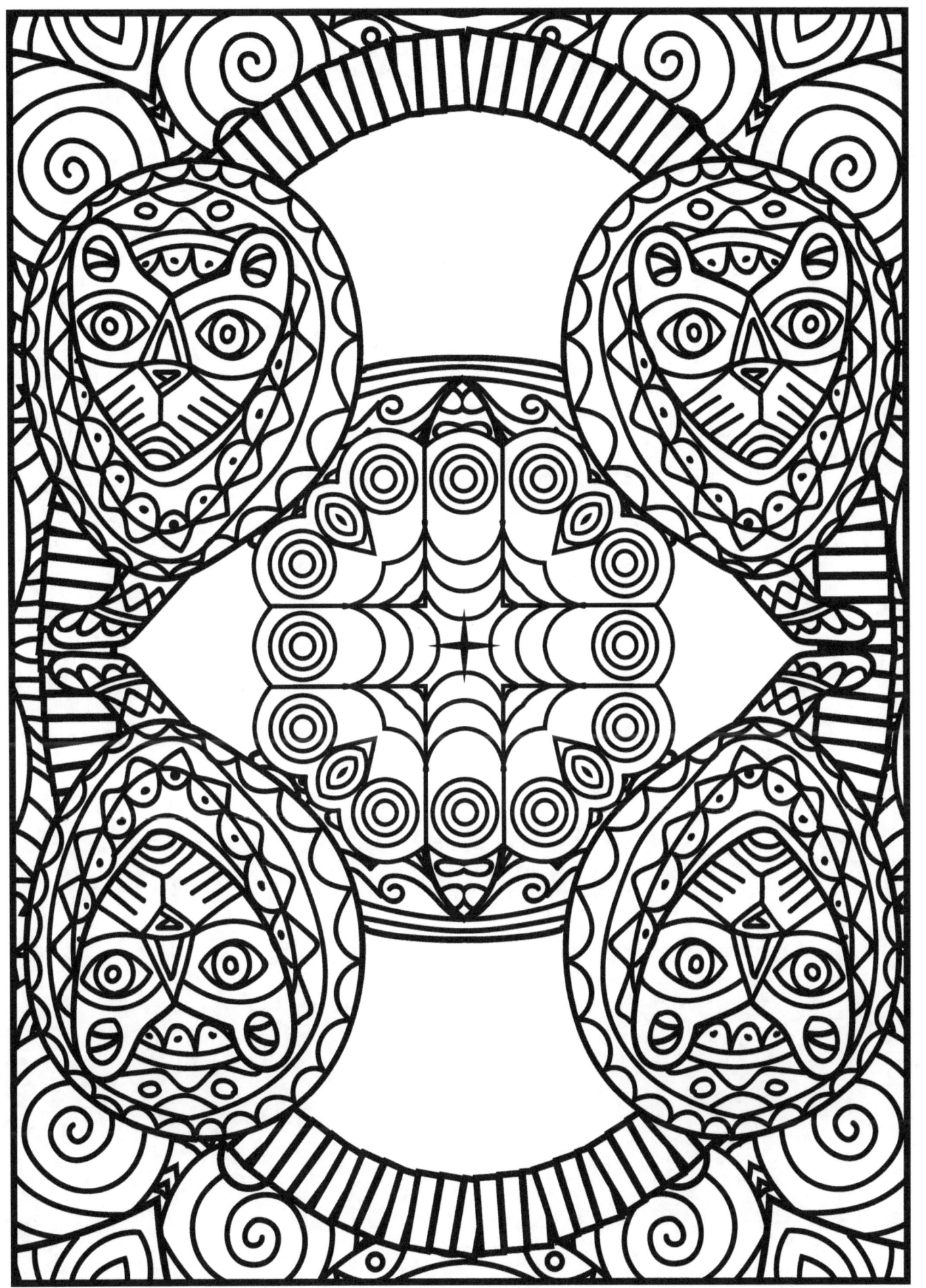

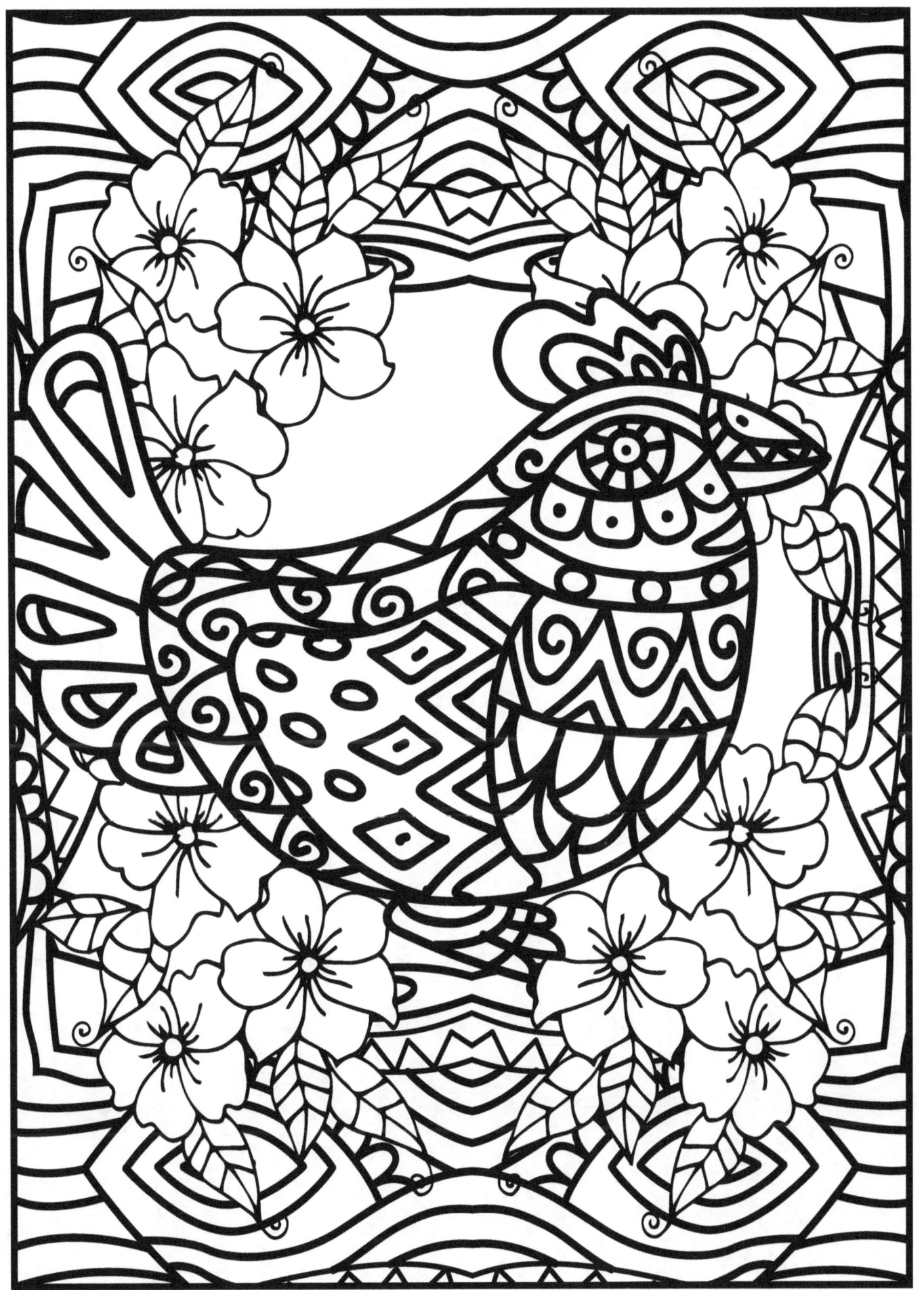

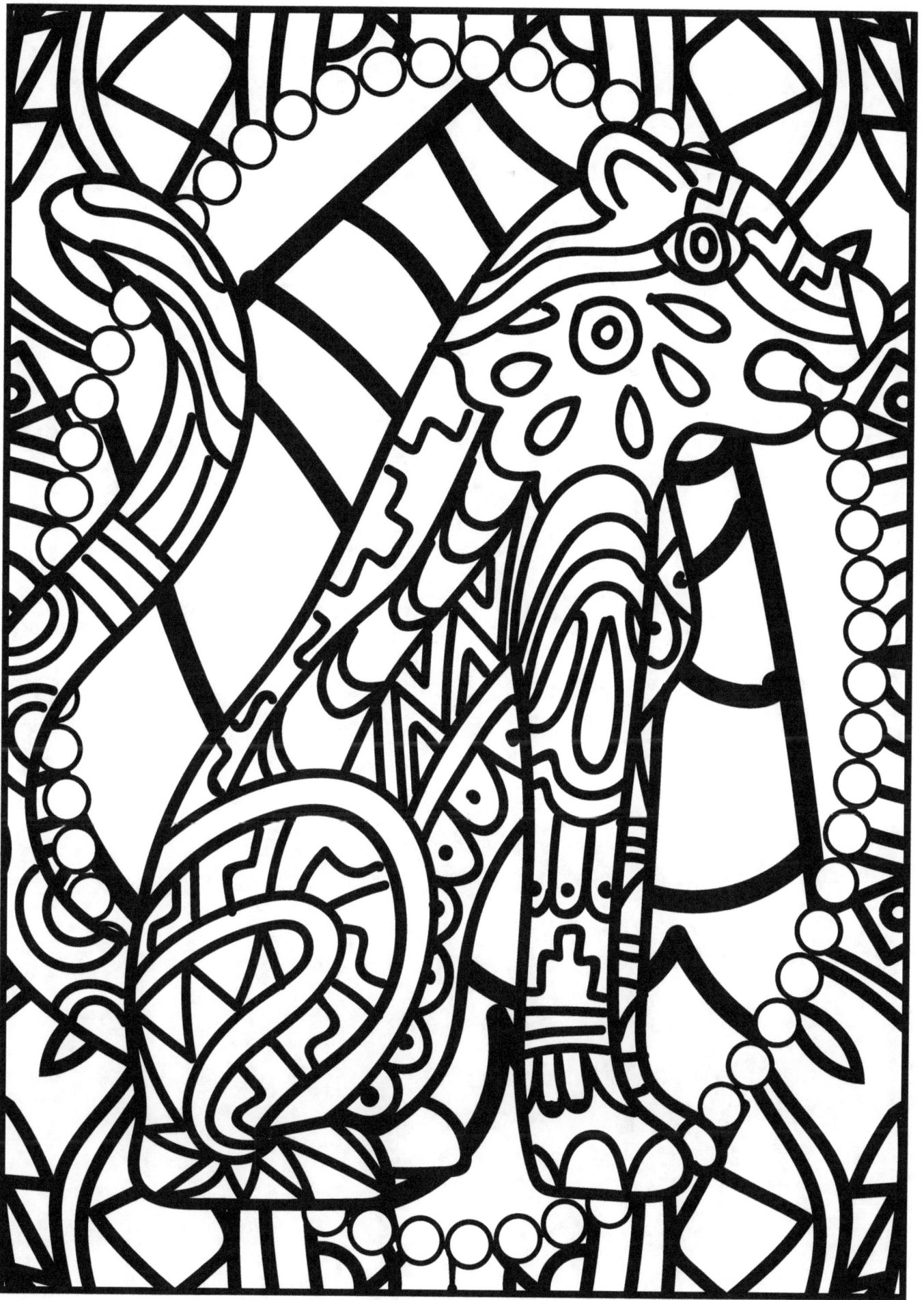

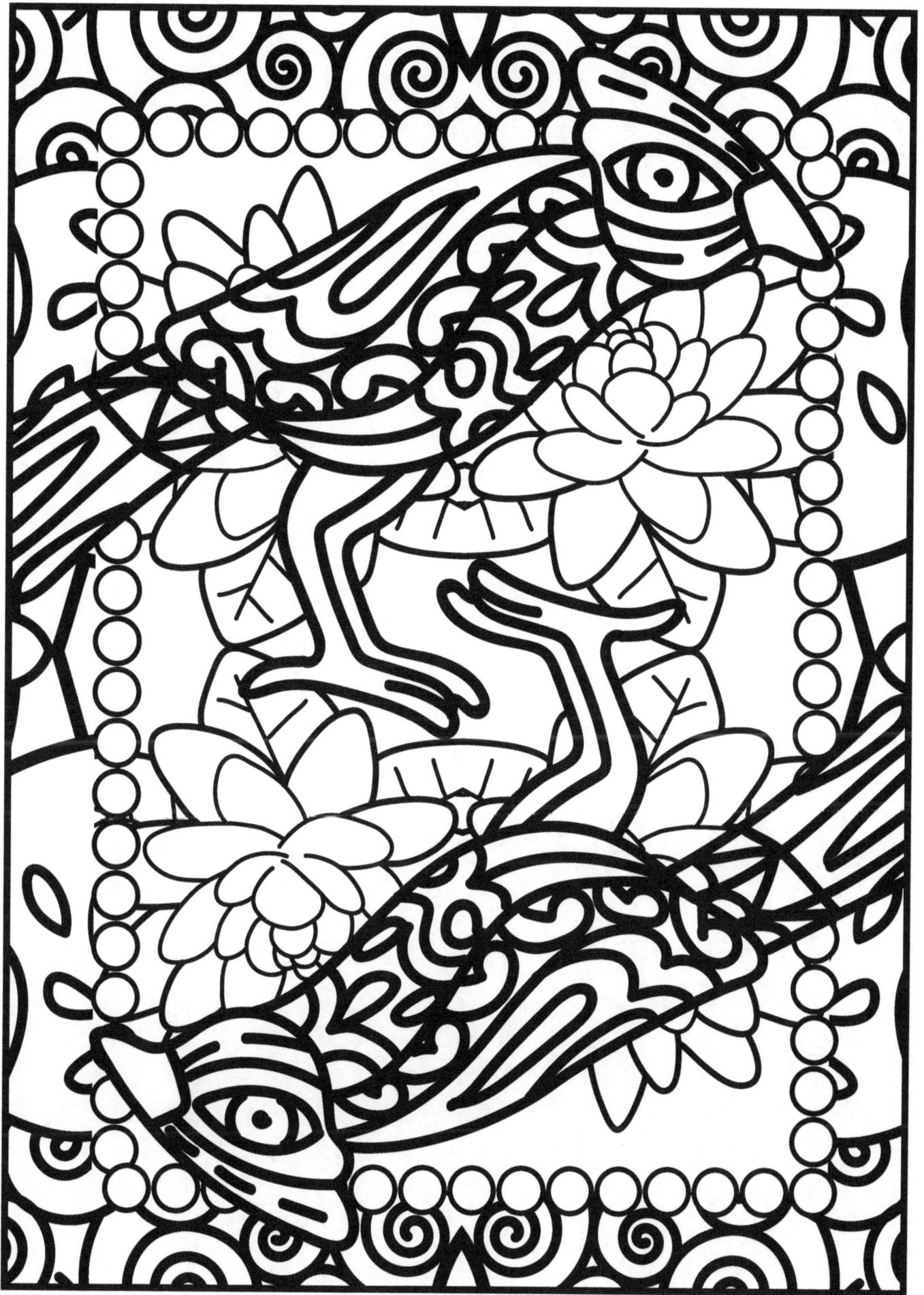

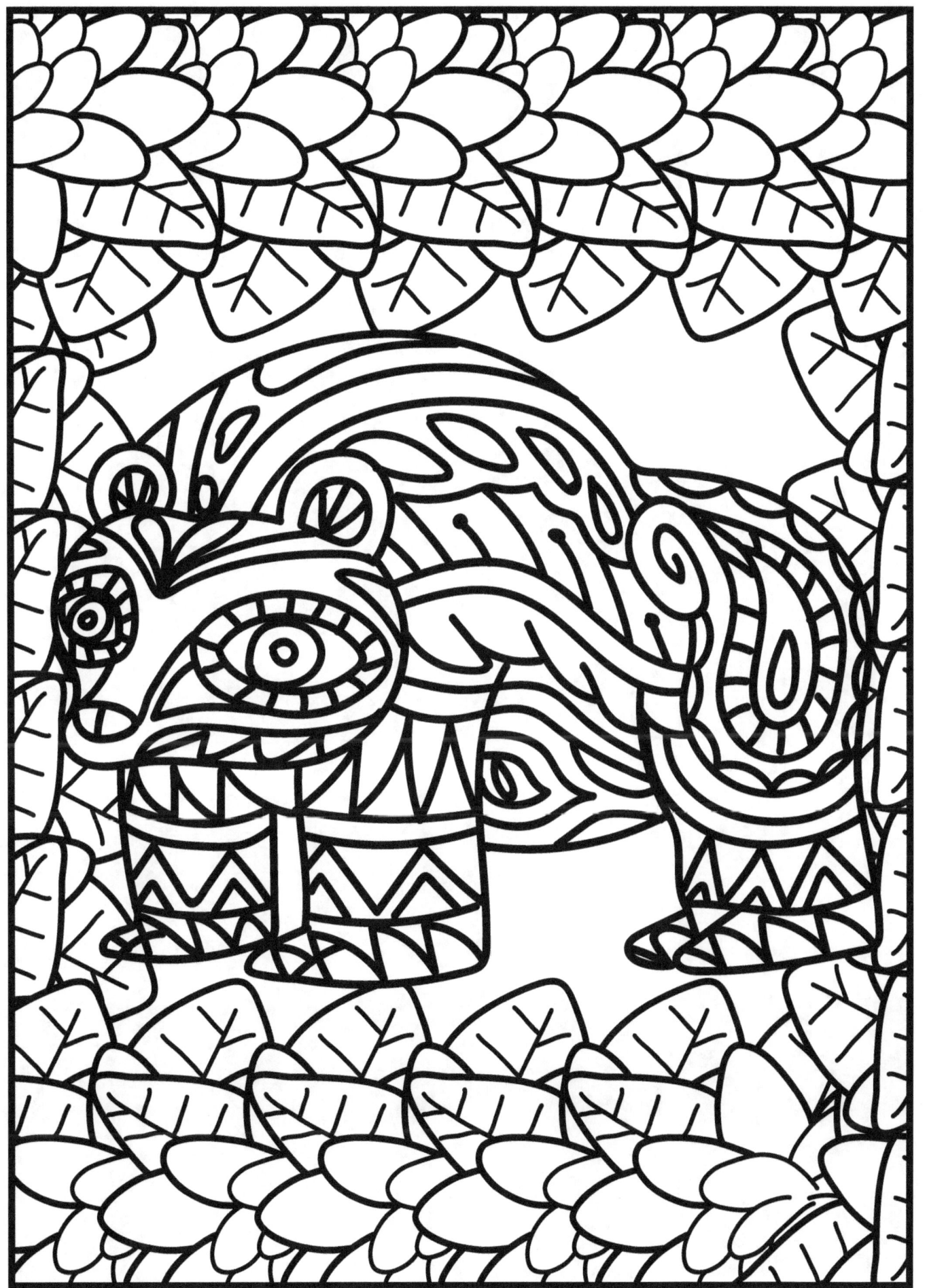

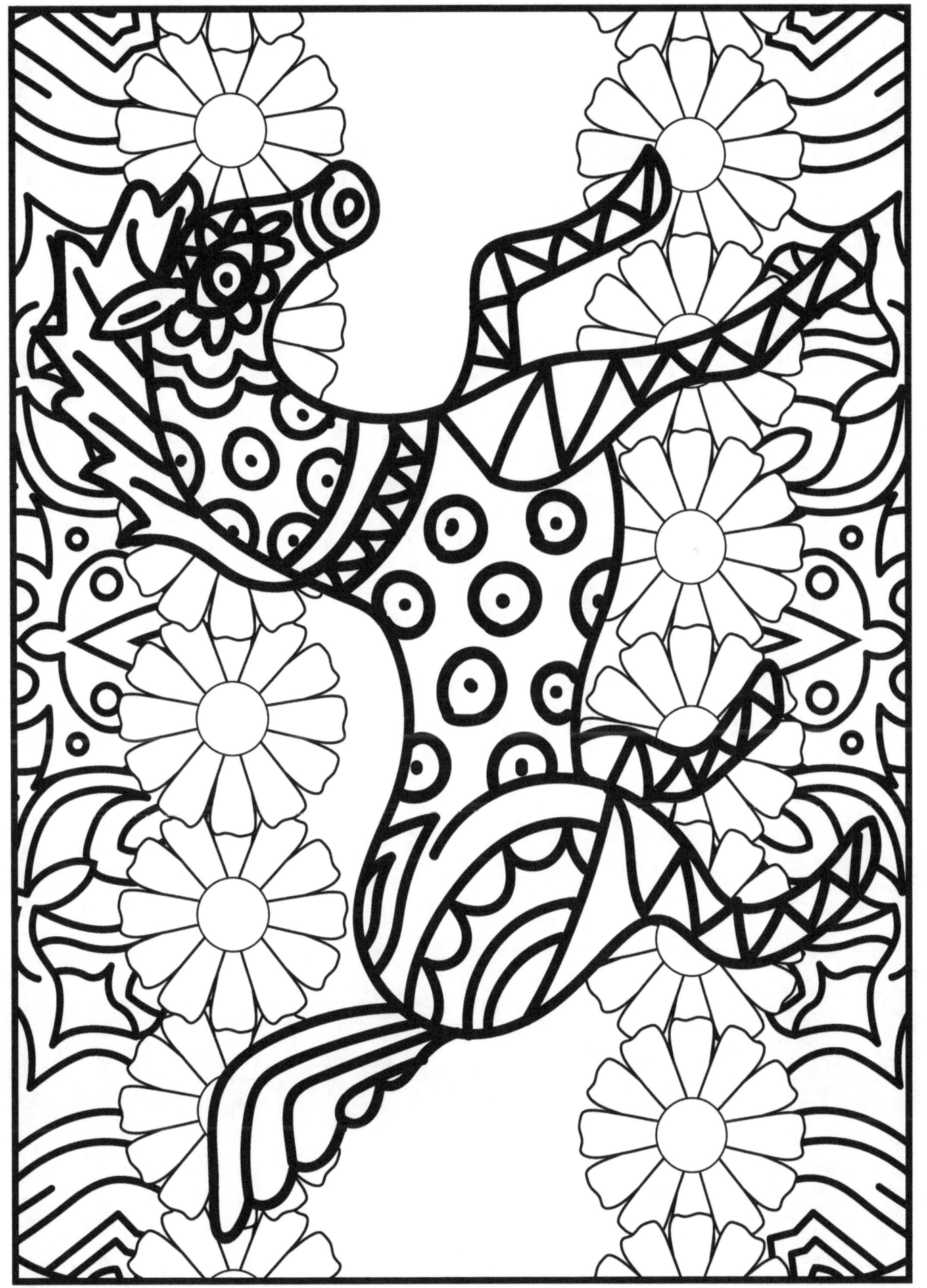

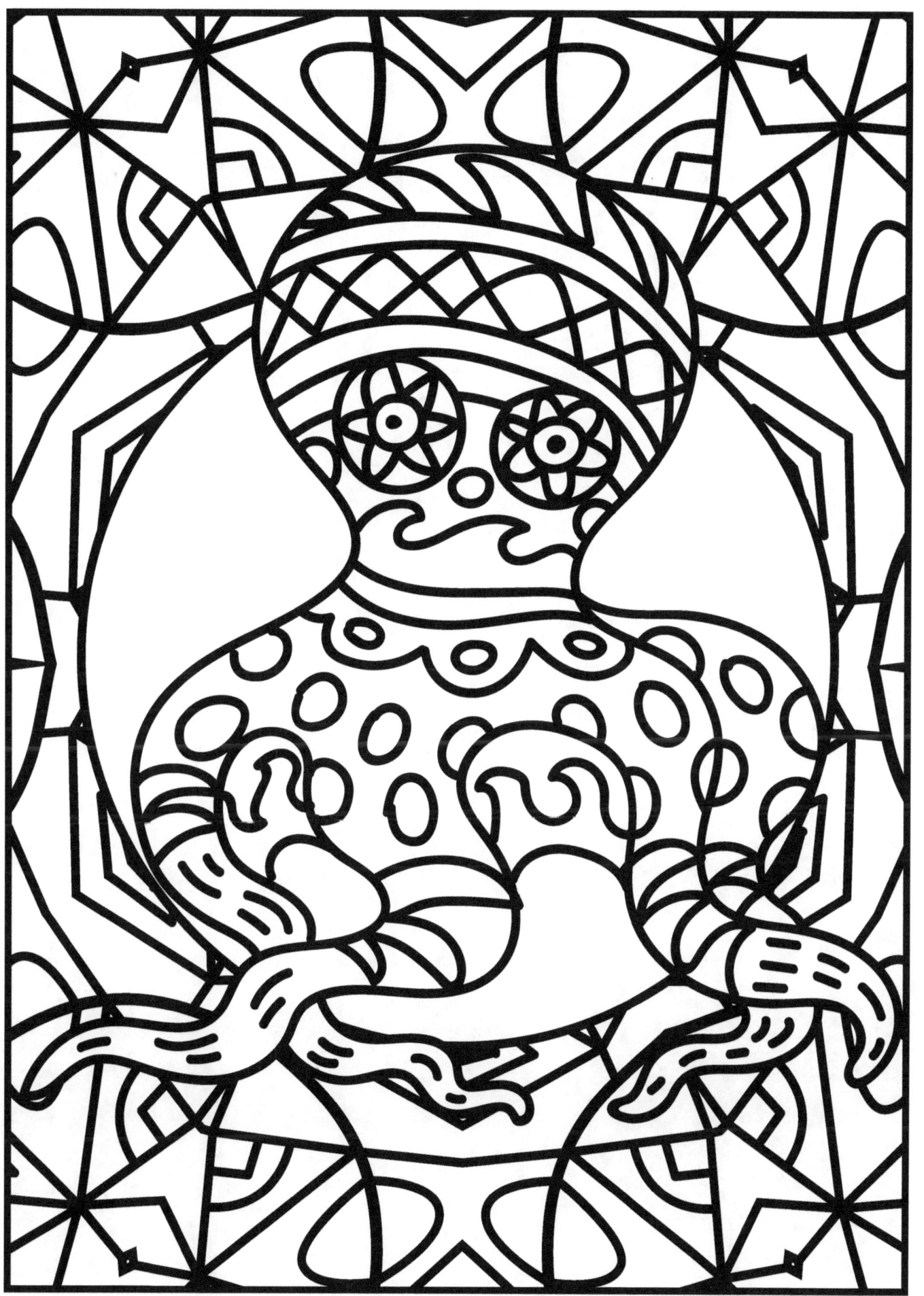

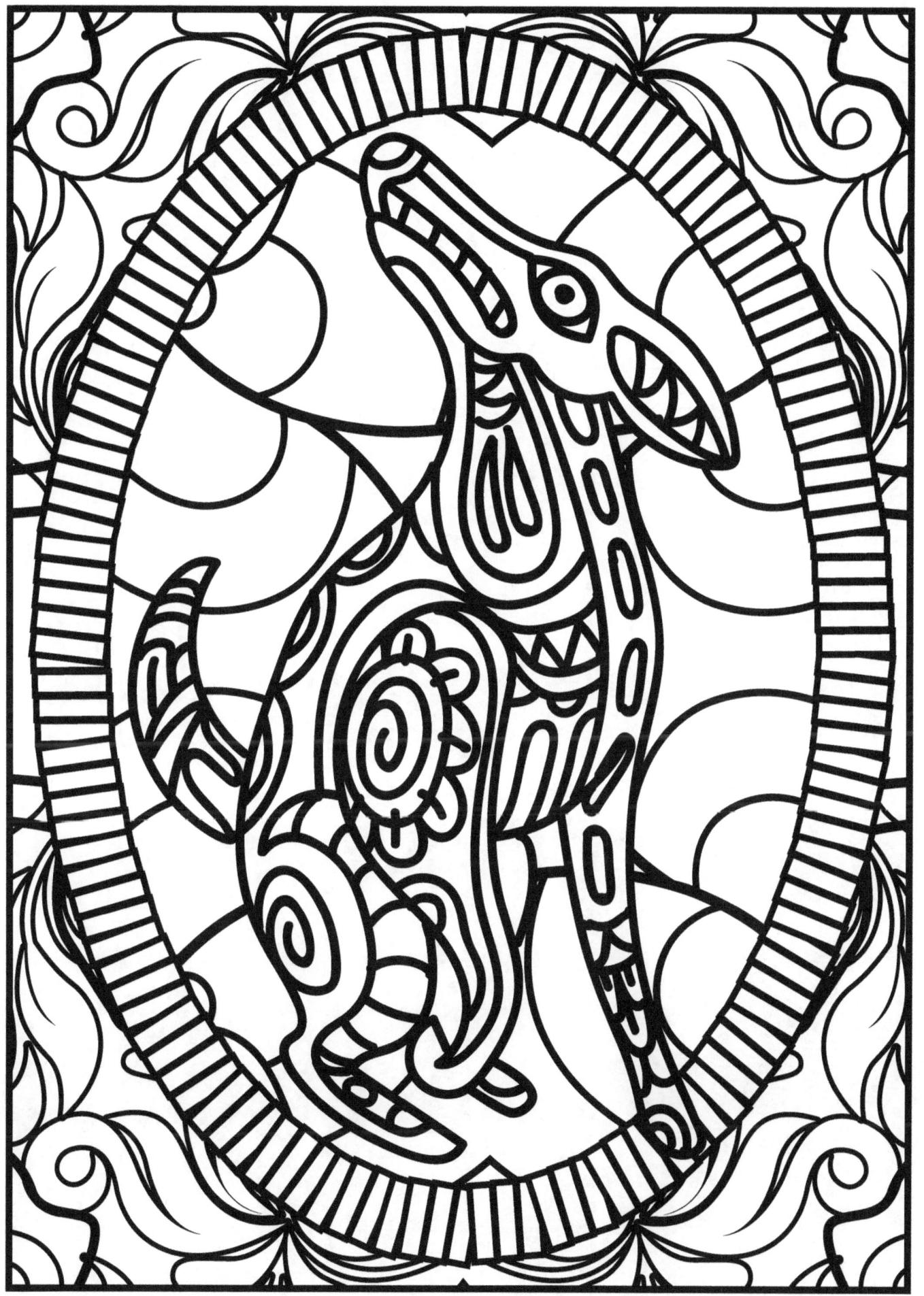

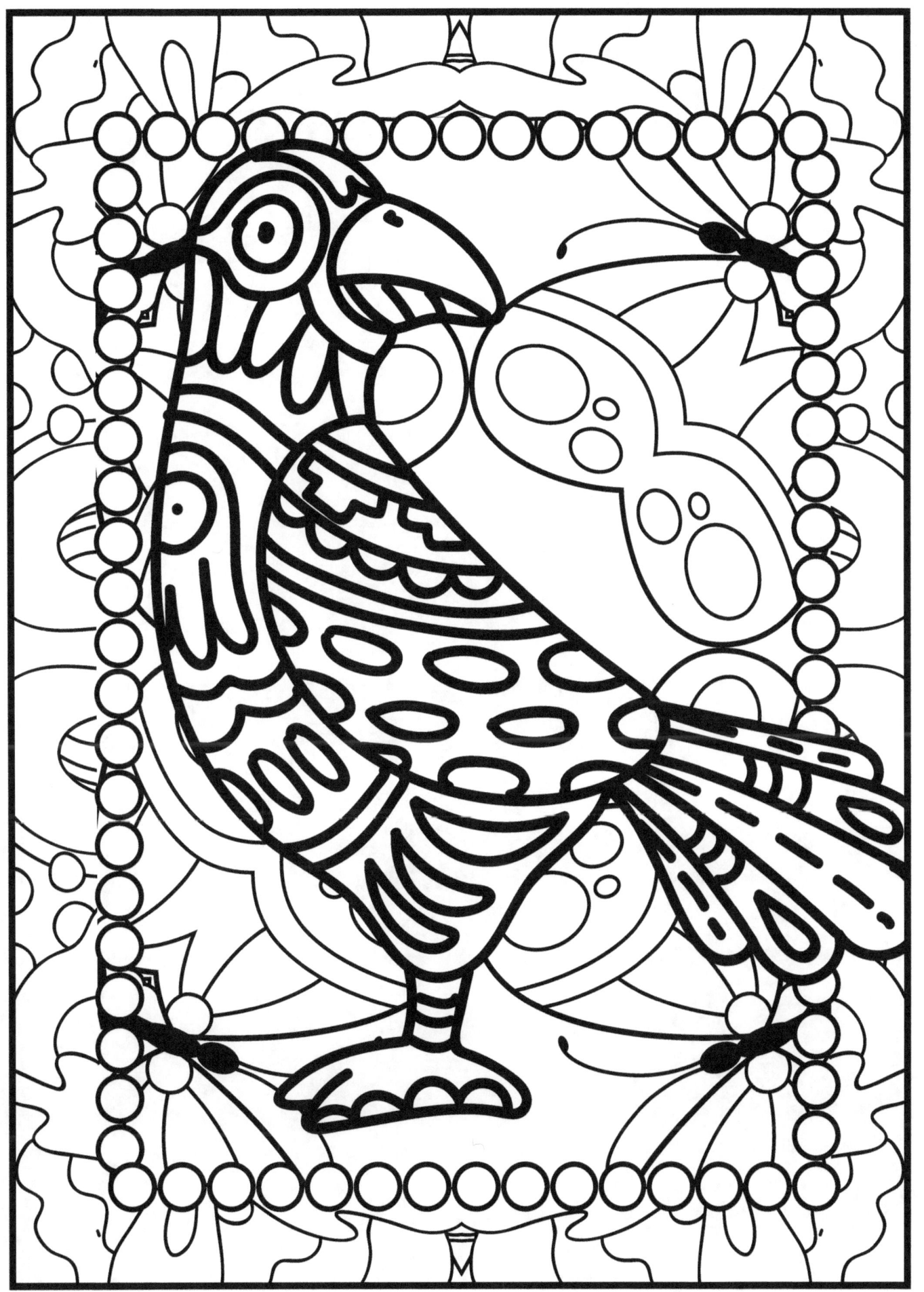

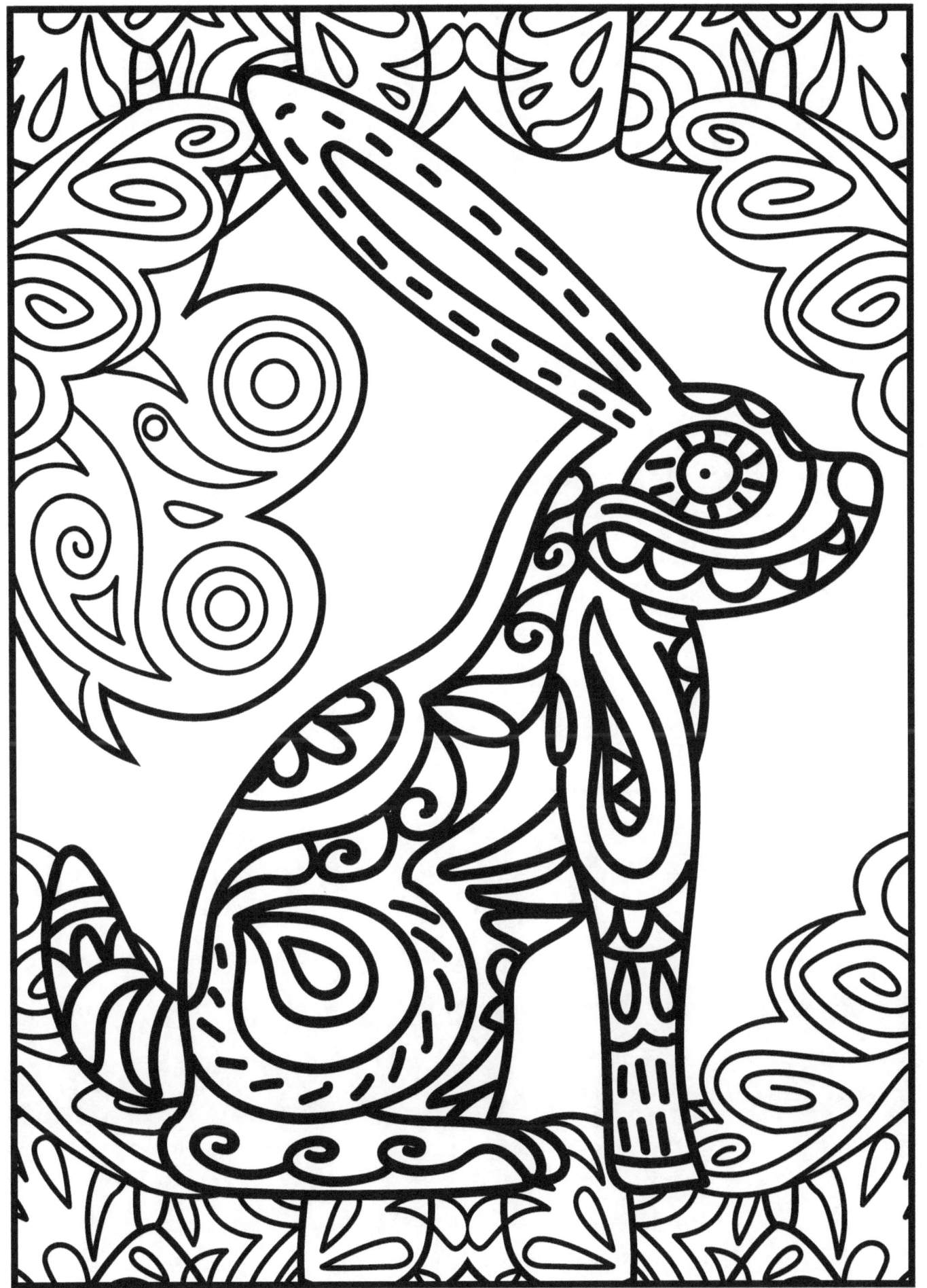

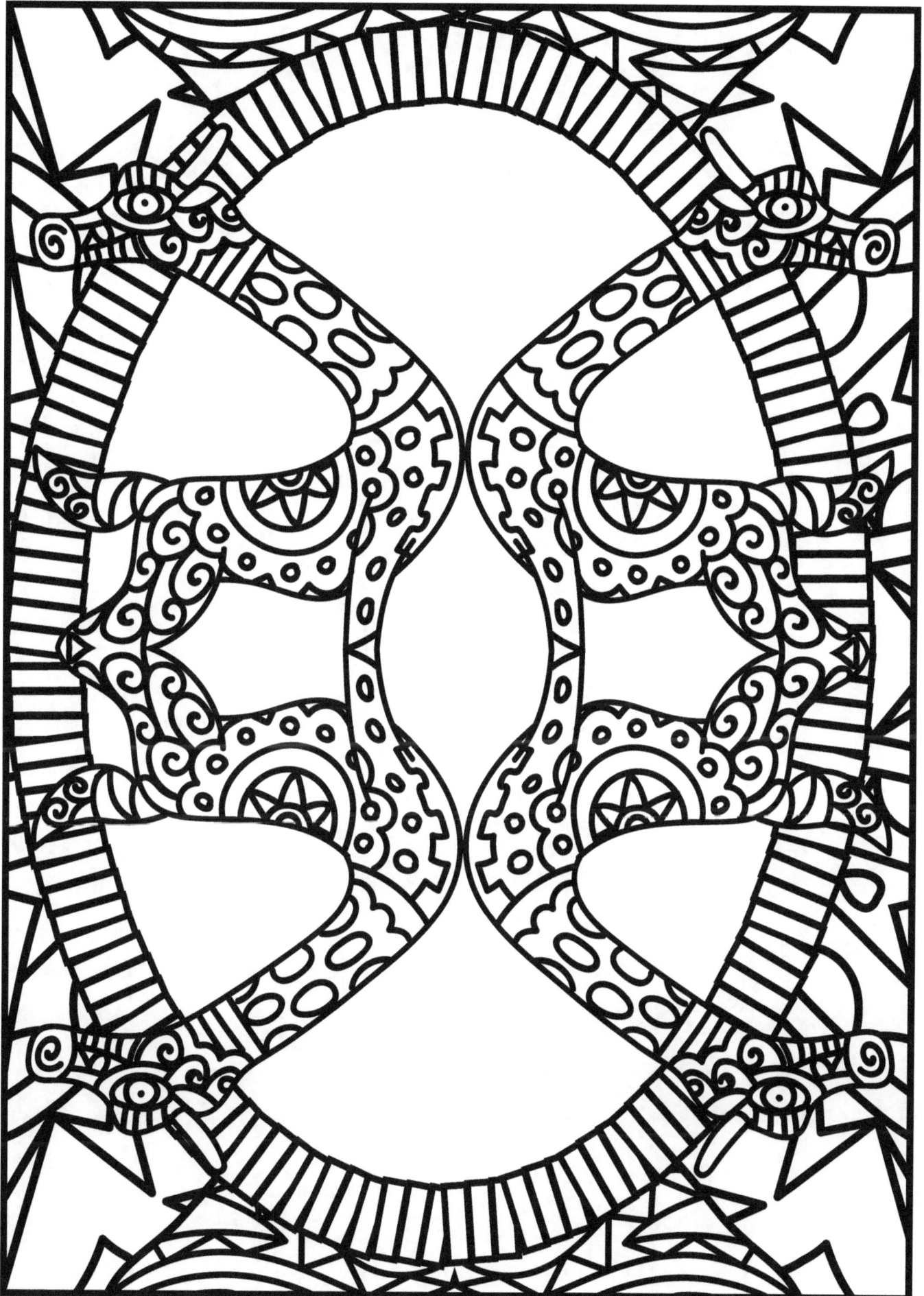

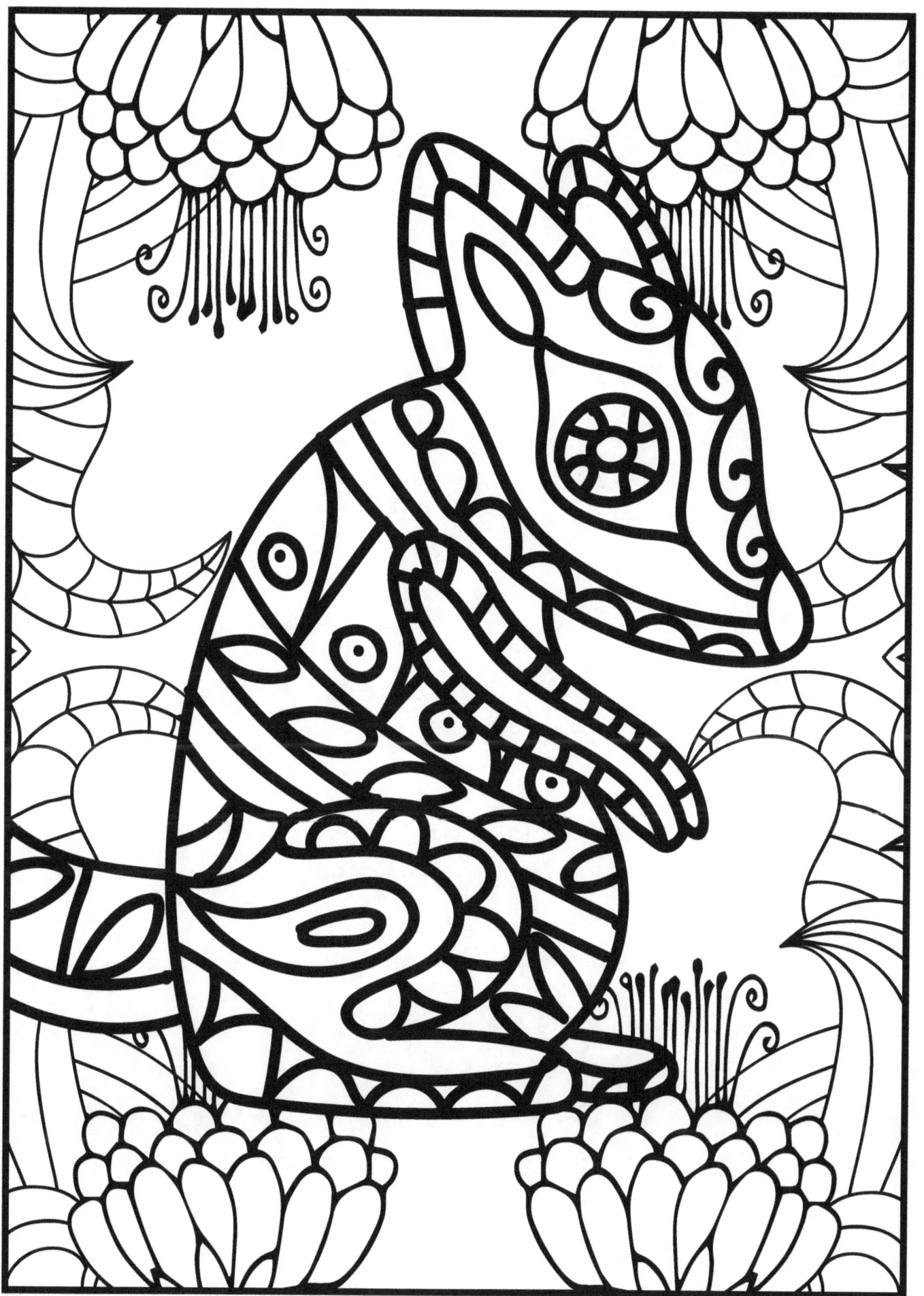

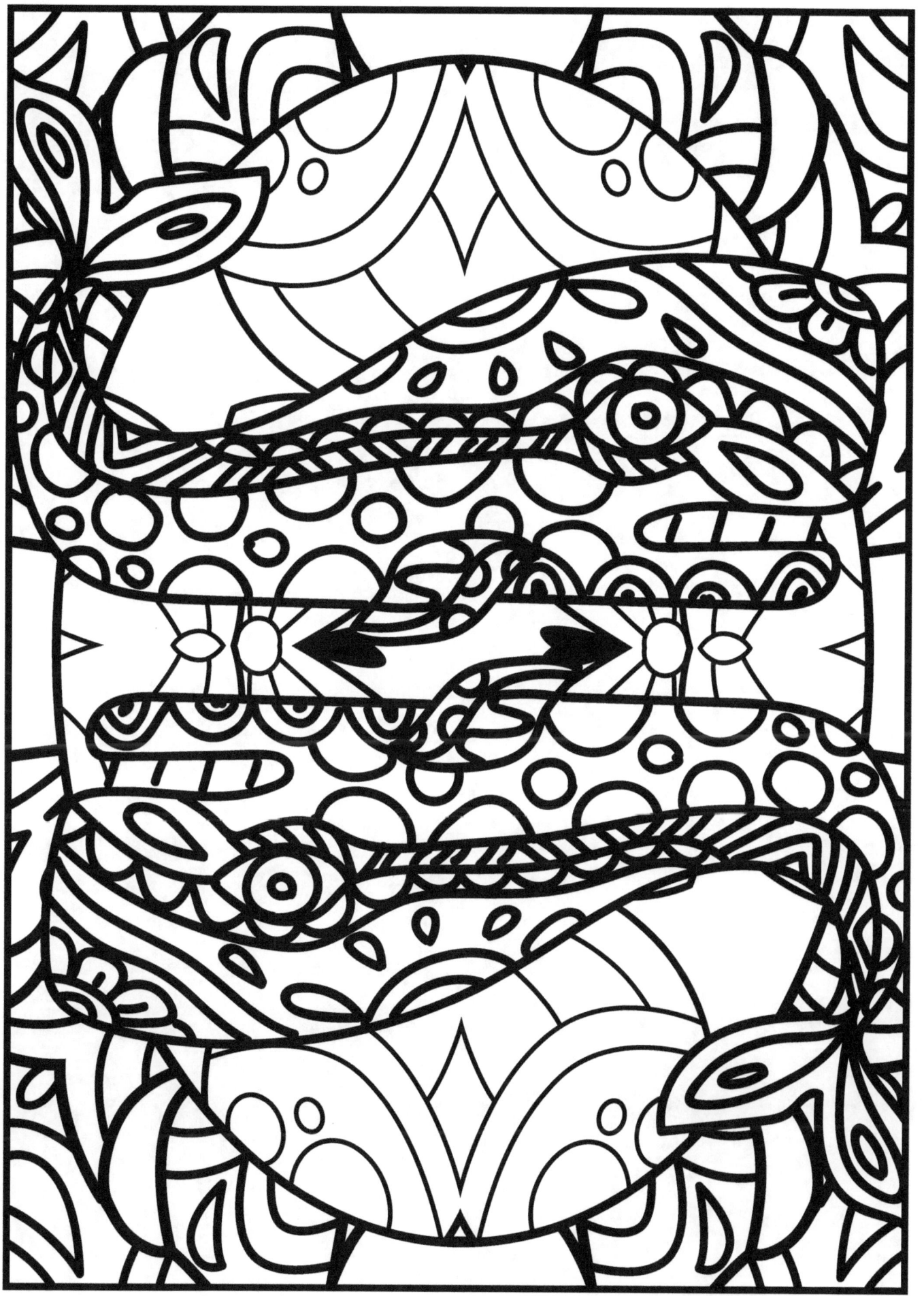

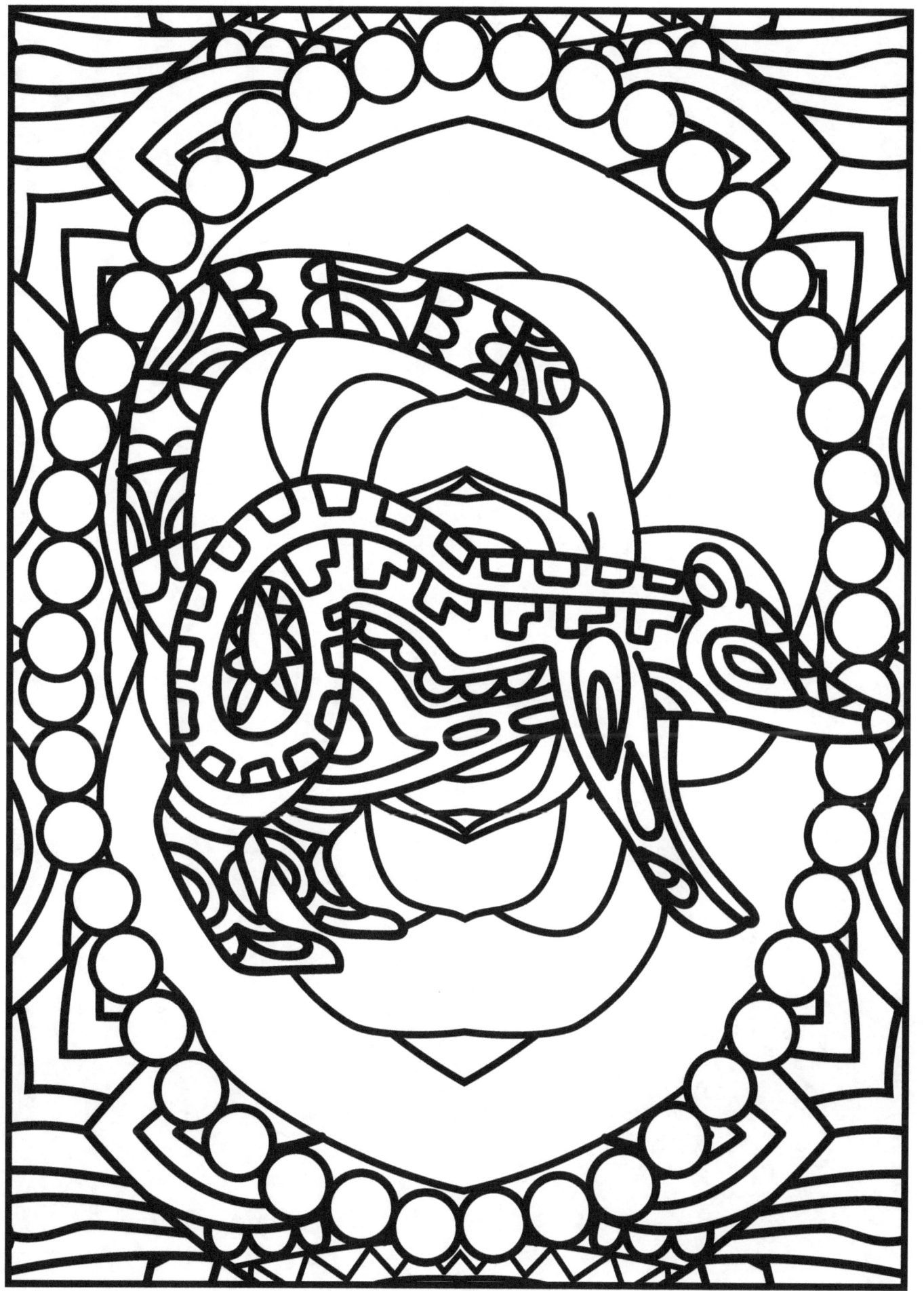

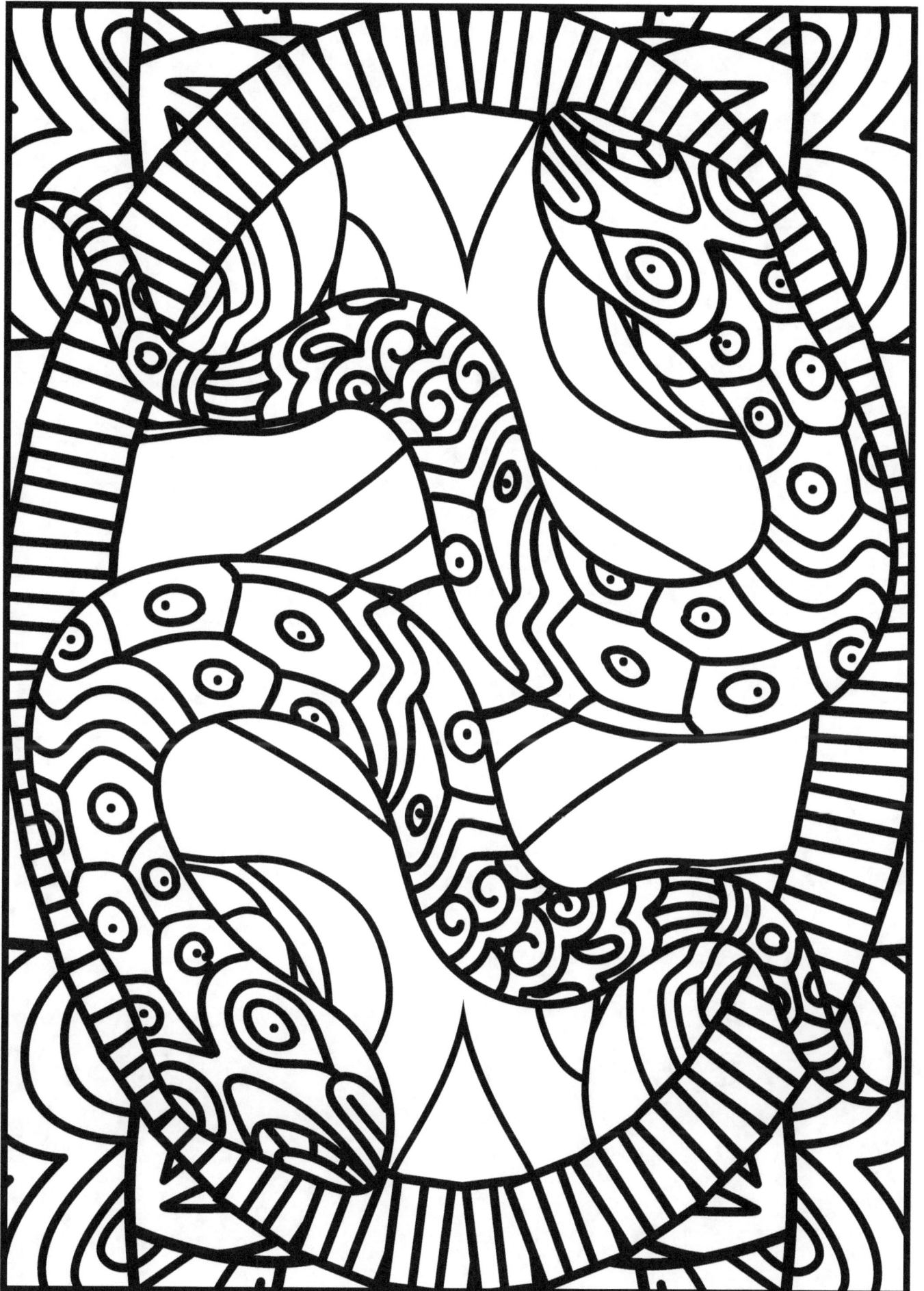

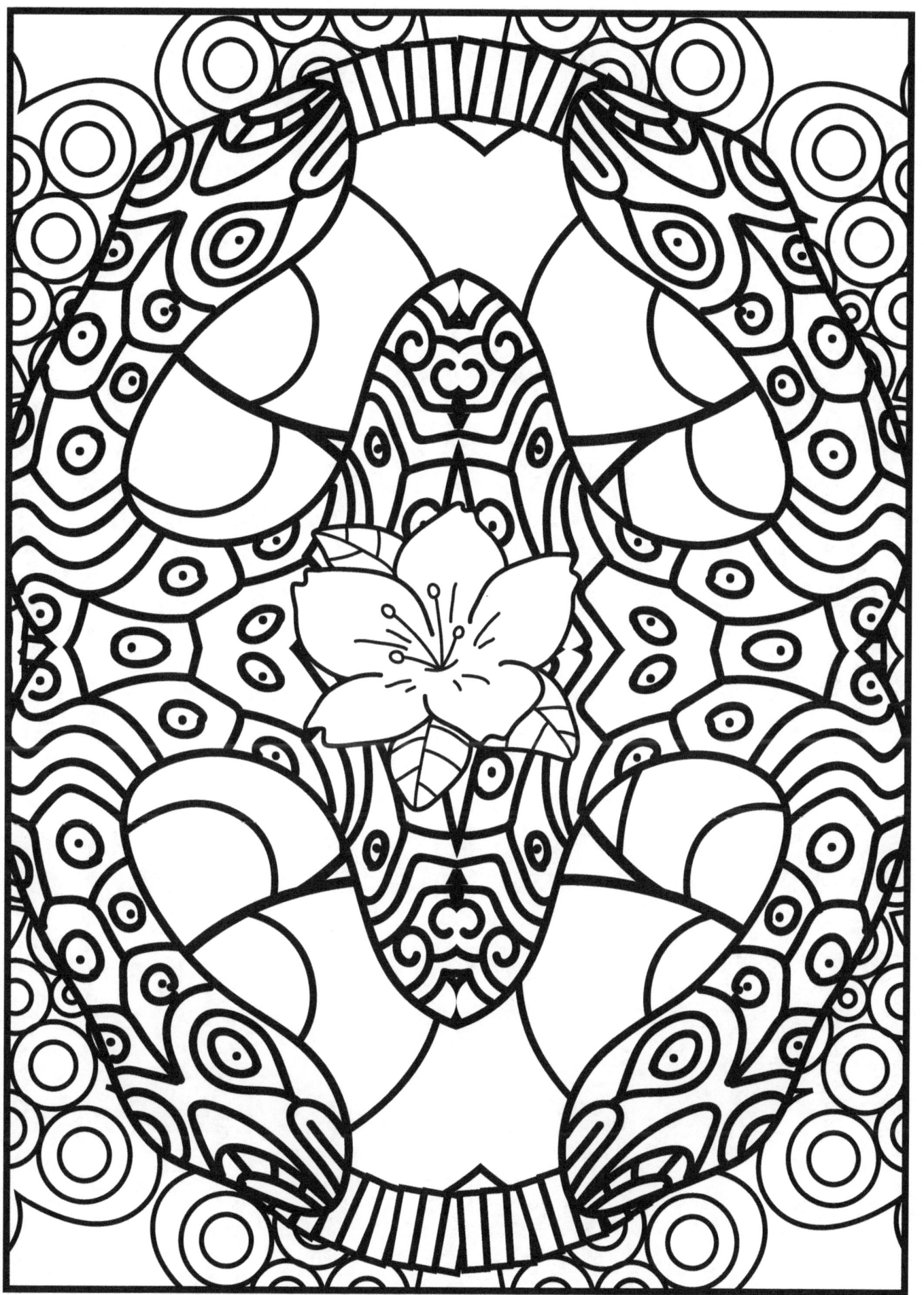

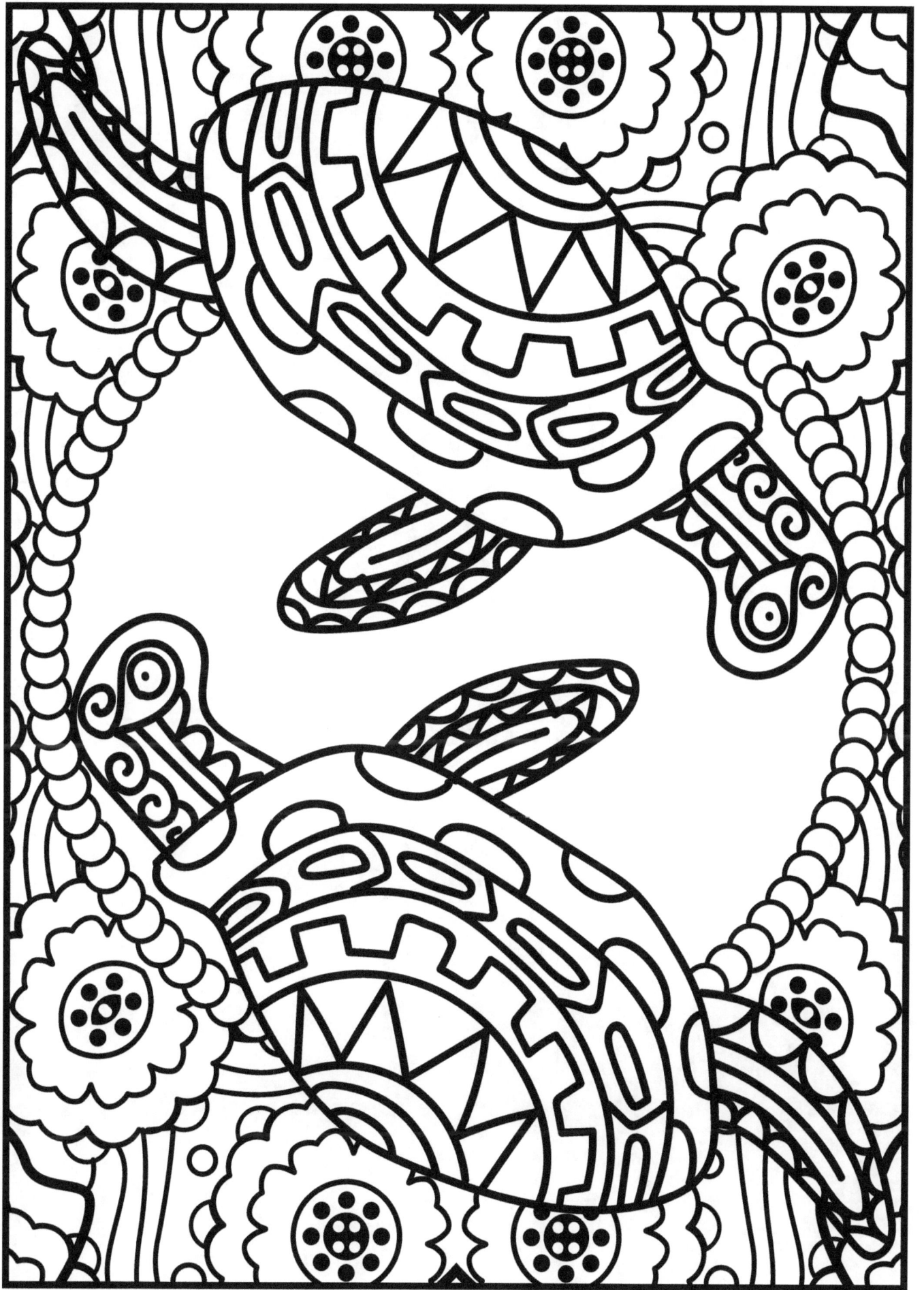

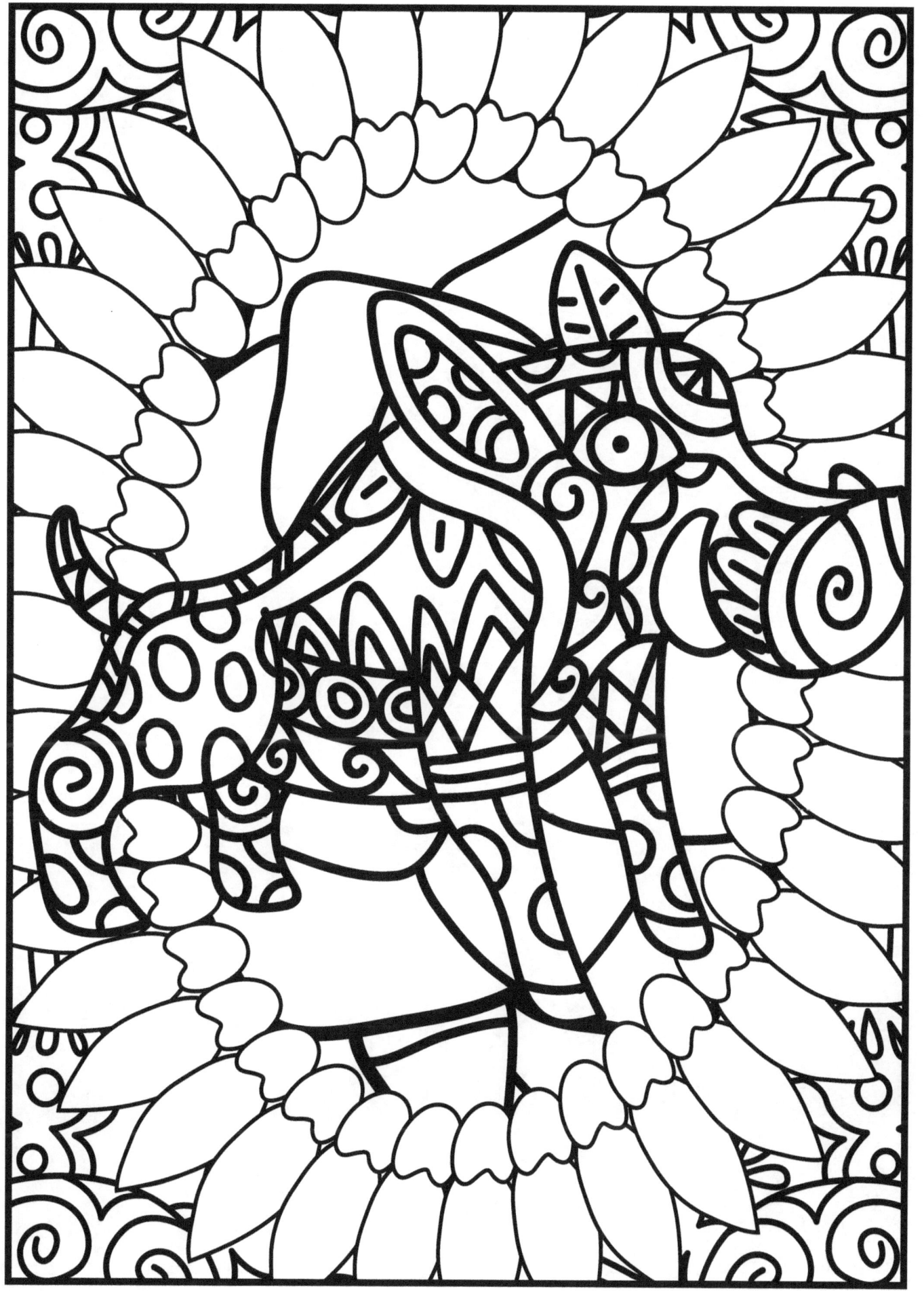

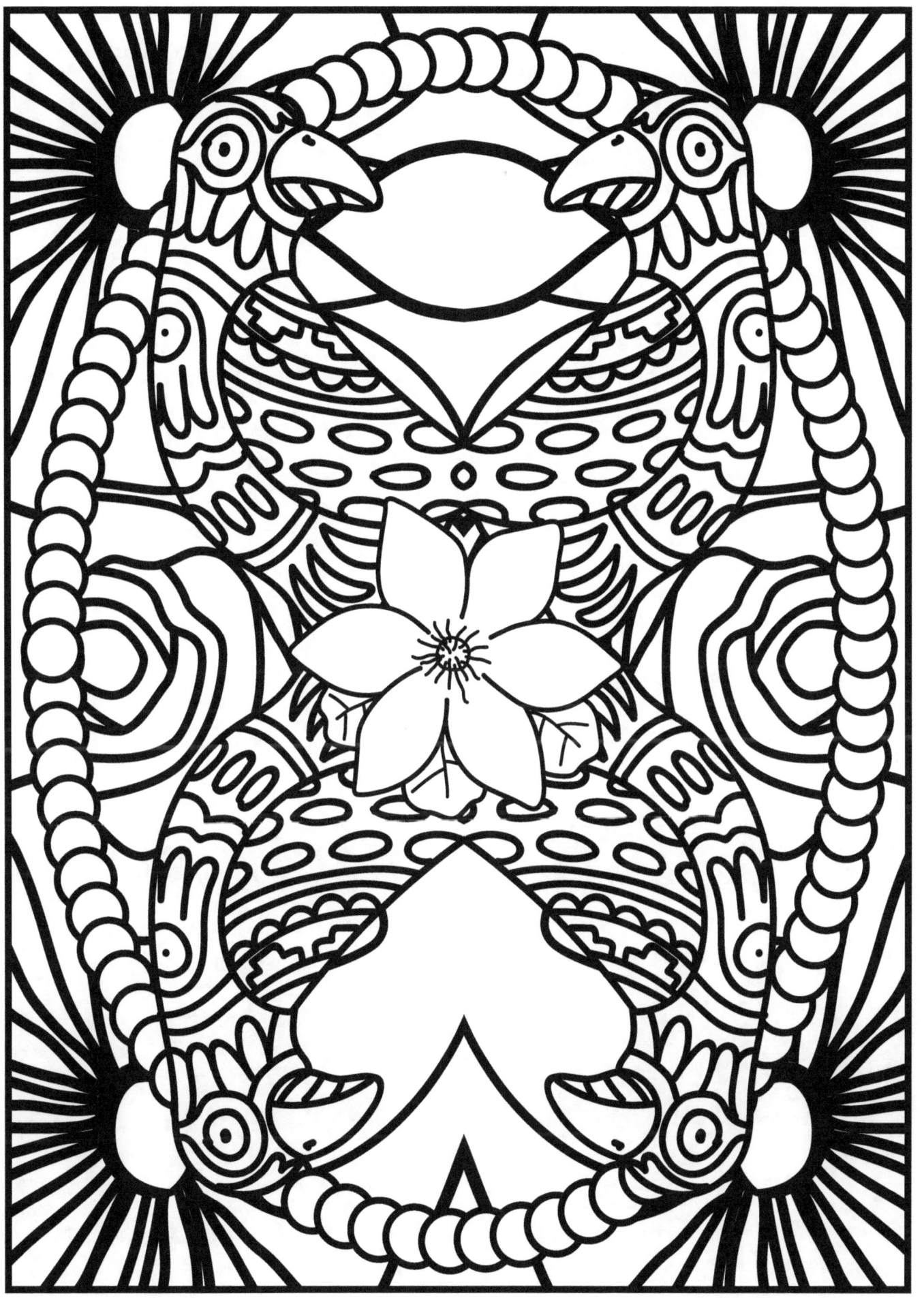

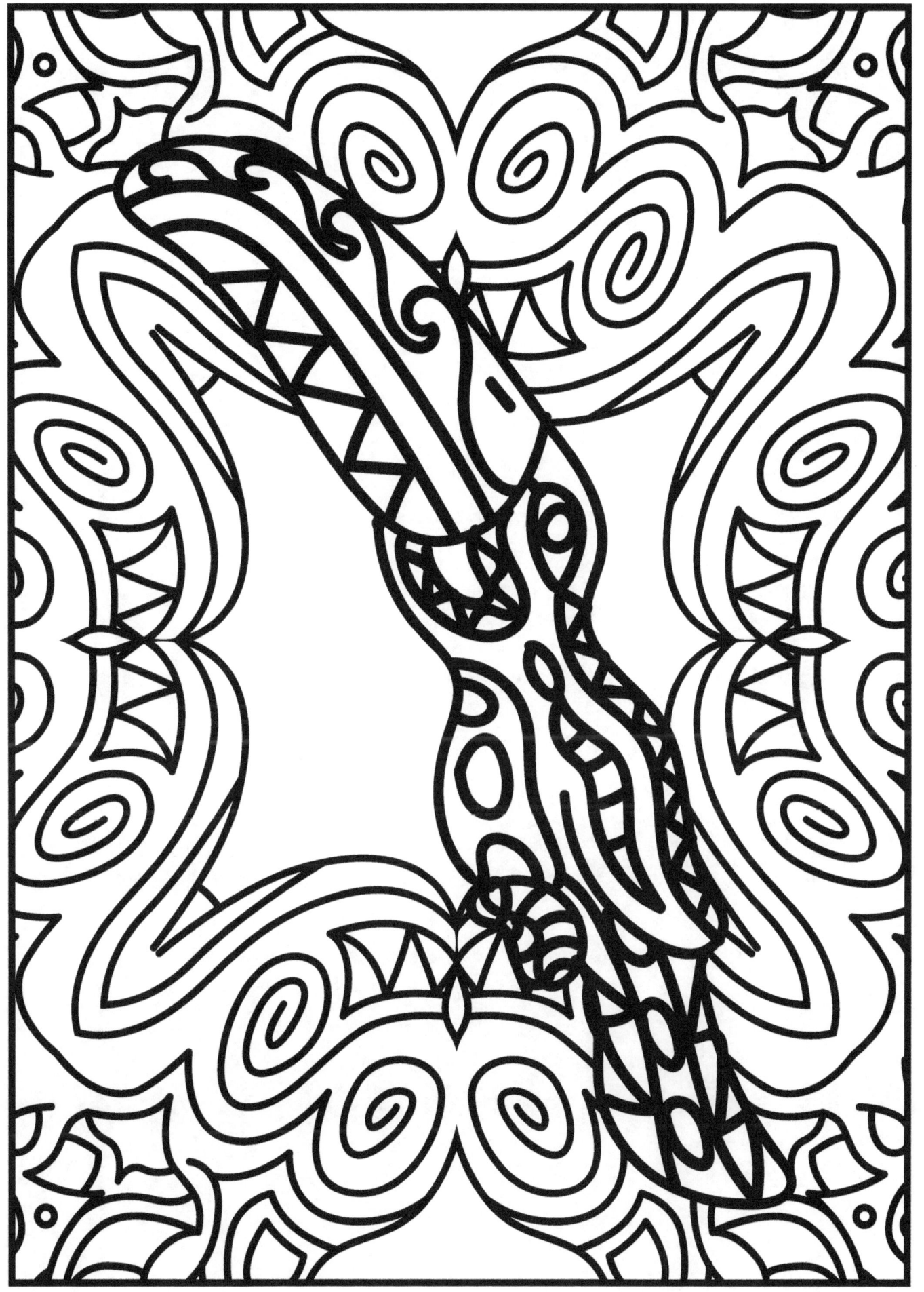

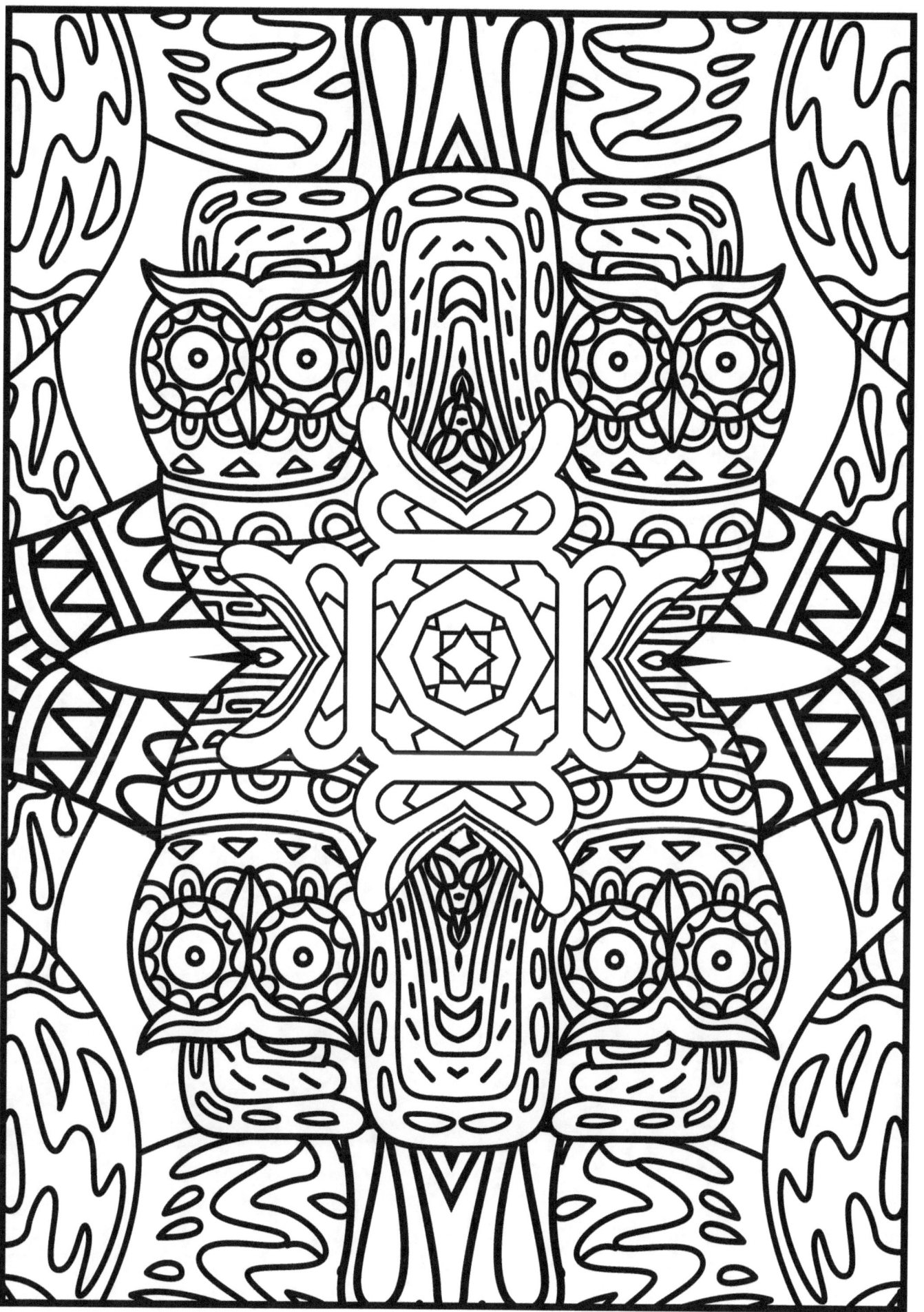

www.ingramcontent.com/pod-product-compliance
Lightning Source LLC
Chambersburg PA
CBHW080622190526
45169CB00009B/3265